Tao

Te

Ching

道
Tao
德
Te
經
Ching

A new translation by
MAN-HO KWOK
MARTIN PALMER
JAY RAMSAY

Calligraphy by
KWOK-LAP CHAN

A catalogue record for this book
is available from the British Library

ISBN 184333-627-8

Cover photograph: The Fairy Magu
by Xiang Gun, British Museum, London

Published by
Vega
64 Brewery Road
London, N7 9NT

A member of Chrysalis Books plc

Visit our website at
www.chrysalisbooks.co.uk

Printed in Italy by Graphicom

Dedications

MAN-HO'S
To my wife, Nancy

MARTIN'S
For Sandra, because I love her

JAY'S
for my father, D. R-B.
and the Age of the Holy Spirit

CONTENTS

INTRODUCTION

WHAT kind of book is the *Tao Te Ching*? In my travels in Chinese society and culture I have seen its texts carved on stone at the tops of holy mountains; painted in gold on sacred scrolls; placed beneath a pregnant woman to ease childbirth; and chanted over a man suffering from psychological distress. I have watched aged Taoist priests pore over it, exploring its depths, and I have watched callow youths from the West stuffing a copy into a rucksack alongside other volumes by writers such as Hesse and Greene.

Of all the books of ancient China, the *Tao Te Ching* has risen to a place of special significance in the West second only to the *I Ching*. In its homeland, China, it is hard to find, having never been as popular amongst ordinary believers as the *T'ai Shang Kan-ying P'ien (The Great One's Book on Response and Retribution)*, a reputed second book by Lao Tzu. In many ways it is not a typical book of Taoist philosophy, lacking humour and containing no stories, unlike other great early 'Taoist' classics such as *Chuang Tzu* and *Lieh Tzu*.

To complicate things even further, it was not written by its reputed author, Lao Tzu, and there is some doubt as to whether Lao Tzu himself ever existed. Supposed to have been written in one night, the *Tao Te Ching* in fact encompasses texts which probably cover a time span of eight hundred years. Seen as the classic of Taoism, it was in use long before Taoism was an identified school. So what exactly is this book, and why is it such a powerful source of inspiration, meditation, guidance, warfare strategy and leadership training? What is the *Tao Te Ching*?

The traditional story of the *Tao Te Ching*'s origin is contained in a biography of Lao Tzu and was first written down at the start of the first century BC by the great historian of China, Ssu-ma Ch'ien. This means it was committed to paper some four hundred years after Lao Tzu was thought to have lived. Ssu-ma Ch'ien found it very difficult to find any firm details about Lao Tzu – a fact which he acknowledges in his book. He states that Lao Tzu was born in Ch'u Jen village in the area of Lai in the Hu Hsien region of the state of Ch'u. His surname was Li, his personal name was Erh and his public or formal name was Tan. Ssu-ma Ch'ien then goes on to claim that Li Erh Tan was the historian of the archives of the state of Ch'u.

Ssu-ma Ch'ien proceeds to record two events in the life of Li Erh Tan. The first is his meeting with Confucius (K'ung Fu-tzu). We know that K'ung was a historical figure. He lived from either 551 or 521 to 479 BC. There is also little doubt that he encountered someone called Lao Tzu, for this meeting is recorded also in Confucian sources. However, the accounts of what happened at this meeting differ somewhat according to whether you read the Confucian or Taoist accounts. The name Lao Tzu should be explained here for those who are wondering what Li Erh Tan has to do with Lao Tzu! Lao Tzu is not a proper name. It is an honorific title and simply means 'the Old Master'. Thus it is impossible to deduce anything from it about the original name of the person to whom it was applied.

According to Ssu-ma Ch'ien, Lao Tzu was a tough old man who had little time for the likes of K'ung. This is Ssu-ma Ch'ien's account of the encounter:

> When K'ung Fu-tzu went to Chou, he asked Lao Tzu to tutor him in the rites. Lao Tzu replied, 'The very bones of those you talk about have turned to dust. All that remains of them is their words. You know that when a noble lives in times which are good, he travels to court in a carriage. But when times are difficult, he goes where the wind blows. Some say that a wise merchant hides his wealth and thus seems poor. Likewise the sage, if he has great internal virtue, seems on the outside to be a fool. Stop being so arrogant; all these demands; your self importance and your overkeen enthusiasm – none of this is true to yourself. That is all I have to say to you.'
>
> K'ung left and said to his followers, 'I know that a bird can fly; that fishes swim; that animals can run. Things that run can be trapped in nets. What can swim can be caught in traps. Those that fly can be shot down with arrows. But what to do with the dragon I do not know. It rises on the clouds and the wind. Today I have met Lao Tzu and he is like the dragon.'

The Confucian account is a little more flattering to K'ung, but retains this image of the wise sage, Lao Tzu, as one who is not trapped by the lure of power, wealth or position.

The only other event recorded by Ssu-ma Ch'ien brings us to the legend of the birth of the *Tao Te Ching*.

Lao Tzu practised the Way and the Virtue (Tao and Te) and his teachings sought to dispel the self. He lived in Chou for a long time, but seeing its corruption, he departed. Upon reaching the Pass, the Keeper who lived there was delighted to see him and asked him, 'As you are just about to leave this world behind you, would you, for my sake, write a book of your thoughts?' In response to this, Lao Tzu wrote a book of two sections, laying out the Way and the Virtue in some five thousand characters, and then departed. He was never seen again and no-one knew where he went.

As with so much else to do with Lao Tzu, this story is not to be taken at face value. In later tellings of the story, Lao Tzu is seen departing towards the West. This gives us a clearer sense of what is almost certainly being hinted at in the Ssu-ma Ch'ien text. The idea of 'travelling West' was that you were going to die. It is this 'departure' that Ssu-ma Ch'ien is hinting at. In later Taoist traditions, especially after the rise of Buddhism in China during the fourth to sixth centuries AD, Taoists also interpreted this text to mean that Lao Tzu went to India. Here, it was claimed, Lao Tzu taught the Buddha everything he knew. Sadly, said the Taoists, the Buddha never could quite get it right! Secondly, whatever else the *Tao Te Ching* is, it is not a book written in one night. Thirdly, the text is longer than five thousand characters – a fact to which we shall return later for it is of some significance. What we have in this lovely story is a picturesque story which means that before he died, the deities (Keepers of the Gate to death) asked Lao Tzu to commit to writing the wisdom for which he was famous.

This story is almost certainly aetiological - that is to say, it explains something which exists now by projecting a story of its origin back to the past. As Ssu-ma Ch'ien discovered over two thousand one hundred years ago, Lao Tzu is a very shadowy figure. If he is, as Ssu-ma Ch'ien claims, both a contemporary of K'ung and of the Tan who was historian of Chou, then he lived a long time, for over one hundred years separate these two people. And if he did write the *Tao Te Ching*, it was not in one night on the edge of the Chinese world.

So who was Lao Tzu and what is his role in the compilation of the *Tao Te Ching*? It is probable that Lao Tzu did exist, but whatever else he did, it is highly unlikely that he compiled the *Tao Te Ching*. He is reputed to have lived around the beginning of the fifth century BC. This period of Chinese history is famous for the variety and range of religio-philosophical teachers, sages and wise men who appeared throughout China. Amongst these there almost certainly was a man who was nicknamed or given the honorific Lao Tzu – 'Old Master'. It is very likely that he may have met K'ung and spoken rather sharply to him. The story is repeated so often, albeit long after the event is supposed to have happened, that there is almost certainly some folk memory at work here. The key to why Lao Tzu became such a hero figure to the Taoists, who emerged as a distinct group only some 300 years later, is contained in the account of this encounter. In it, as the quote shows, K'ung was firmly put down and his worldly philosophy and concerns were mocked. Furthermore, Lao Tzu spoke of the superiority of the sage who knows the true path and values in life.

Lao Tzu is shown as being the complete opposite of K'ung. As such it is natural that teachings and insights which radically differed from the norms of Confucian thought and practice should have been attributed to this sage figure who had so firmly put K'ung in his place. Essentially, Lao Tzu became a convenient figure around whom to group sayings which countered the prevailing Confucian wisdom. This did not happen overnight. Far from it. Nor was the material which collected around this enigmatic figure all created after his death. For in the materials which gradually came to form the *Tao Te Ching* are sections which are much older than the fifth century BC – sections which date from hundreds of years before the time of Lao Tzu.

To have some appreciation of the sorts of materials which merged into the *Tao Te Ching*, it is important to look at some of the strands which flowed into the formation of a self-conscious Taoism which emerged somewhere around 300 BC.

One of the most ancient strands of Taoism is shamanism. This, reputedly the oldest world faith, spread from its original heartland of Siberia some eight thousand years ago. From Siberia it spread across the landbridge then linking Alaska to Siberia. It spread down through North America into South America. It also spread south into China, Japan and Korea and on from there to South East Asia: at its core is a belief that there are two worlds. The material, physical world which we experience, and a superior world, the spiritual world which exists beside this world and sometimes breaks in to affect this world. The role of the shaman, the key figure in this faith, is to be able to contact the other world, to be in touch with the forces which affect this world and to either pacify them or to call upon their aid. The shaman goes into a trance whereby he or she is able to move between the worlds and to answer questions or seek help. This idea of the shaman being in touch with the world of the spirit is what lies behind the Taoist notion of the sage being able to flow with the true natural forces of the universe. Shamanism also sees certain creatures and places within the natural world as being more open or receptive to the forces of the other world than others and this is where the idea of the sage in retreat and the reverence for certain animals within Taoism are also to be found.

The shamanists in China continued to exercise considerable influence for hundreds if not thousands of years. Their role in Chinese society is detectable down through all periods of history, until they eventually re-emerged in a new form as the 'priests' of what is called religious Taoism, which arose in the second century AD. To this day, shamanistic practices continue in many parts of rural China, usually taking place under the umbrella terms of either folk Taoism or folk religion.

Part of the shamanistic role was the ability to be a vehicle for oracles and for divinational messages. This is one of the features of the shamans who are recorded in both the histories and the poetry of the period from the fifth century BC to the first century AD, where we find shamanistic figures functioning in the courts of ancient China. The importance of this for the *Tao Te Ching* is that within some of its chapters are captured, like flies in amber, shamanistic oracles and divinational messages similar, and in one or two cases, identical, to those found within the greatest of oracle books, the *I Ching*.

Another strand within Taoism and within the *Tao Te Ching* is the philosopher sage. During the fifth and sixth centuries BC, China experienced one of the most dramatic upsurges of religio-philosophical activity the world has ever seen. Indeed, so prolific was this outpouring of wisdom and teachings that it is known in Chinese as the era of the 'Hundred Schools' (that is schools of thought). The philosopher sage also owes his origins to the shaman. The shaman was frequently consulted by the king in matters of government and rule – hence some of the oracles which are to be found within the *Tao Te Ching*. But the shaman had at an even earlier time often been the actual ruler.

This tradition of the sage/ruler is captured in the earliest legends of the Three August Ones and the Five August Rulers. These shadowy and at times very strange figures are dated to the third millenium BC. They all have aspects of both priest and ruler about them, combining shamanistic powers with worldly rule. For instance, there is Fu Hsi, the first of the Three August Ones, dated to around 3000 BC. Fu Hsi is described as being part human and part animal – in itself a reflection of the most powerful form of shaman. To this day, certain shamanistic communities believe that their shamans are animals, such as bears, who can transform themselves from one shape to another at will. The standard description of the skills of Fu Hsi is given in the *Great Treatise of the I Ching*. It says:

When in ancient times Fu Hsi ruled the world, he looked up to observe the phenomena of the heavens, and gazed down to observe the contours of the earth. He observed the markings of birds and beasts and how they adapted to their habitats. Some ideas he took from his own body, and went beyond this to take other ideas from other things. Thus he invented the eight trigrams in order to comprehend the virtues of spiritual beings and represent the conditions of all things in creation.

Here we see the fusion between ruler, wise man, mystic, communicator and harmoniser between different worlds – the roles of the shaman ruler. In the *Tao Te Ching* we have strong echoes of this in the sage/ruler who is both spoken of and occasionally speaks – see in particular Chapters 3 and 17. The sage/ruler flows with the way of nature – is in touch with the greater spirit world. He guides the people, though they hardly realize it, and he acts in accord with what is right. In this image of the sage/ruler we have very ancient elements within the text of the *Tao Te Ching*, elements which came to coalesce around the mysterious figure of Lao Tzu.

In asking what kind of a book the *Tao Te Ching* is, we have to acknowledge that at many levels it is not a very 'Taoist' book – according to what most people understand Taoism to be. Taoism, certainly since the second century AD, has been a mixture of folk religion combining magic, liturgies, ritual and deities, alongside the more philosophical ideas of the Taoist recluse, living simply in the depths of the forest or high on a remote mountain. The obsession with achieving immortality is one of the factors which spans both these groups. Yet the *Tao Te Ching* is devoid of almost all of this. There is no magical formula within the text, even though the *Tao Te Ching* is more often than not used and interpreted today by Chinese believers as being a powerful book of charms. There is not really the idea of the remote sage. Instead we have the engaged sage: the ruler sage who offers advice on such apparently un-Taoist activities as military cunning, political manoeuvring and inter-state diplomatic policies. It contains not a single

mention of a deity nor does it offer a creed or set of beliefs other than certain broad principles and a structured cosmology.

We even have difficulty translating the name! *Tao Te Ching* means 'the Way, the Virtue Classic'. *Ching* is a title given to any book which is considered to be a classic, and whilst the *Tao Te Ching* was only very briefly considered one of the major formal classics of ancient China (during the T'ang dynasty 618 to 906 AD), it has long carried this title. It seems to have been first applied during the Han dynasty (207 BC to 220 AD). But what exactly does the Way, the Virtue, mean? Is it, as Arthur Waley translated it, 'the Way and its Power'? Or is it better translated as 'the Virtue of the Tao', as Joseph Needham puts it? Increasingly nowadays, translators just leave it in the Chinese – the *Tao Te Ching*.

Whatever else the *Tao Te Ching* is or is not, there can be no question that it is one of the most important books in Chinese literature. Its influence has been felt throughout all the centuries since the Han dynasty and its influence on Western society is second to none in terms of non-Western books. Titles like Fritjof Capra's *The Tao of Physics* illustrate the way in which this remarkable book has penetrated, at one level or another, into Western thought. Perhaps it is time now to look at what the book is – to discover that its history and its contents are even more fascinating than has previously been thought, and to see that in discovering its origins, we have to engage in historical detective work.

The *Tao Te Ching* is not a book in the conventional sense that we understand. It is a collection of sayings and commentaries, usually unconnected with that which comes before and that which comes after. The best way to see its eighty-one chapters is as a set of pearls, each one perfectly rounded, strung on a string. Like pearls, they are individual and separate, yet the overall effect is that of a beauty and a pattern which unites them.

The reason for this is that the chapters in the *Tao Te Ching* show all the signs of being separate wisdom teachings which have been passed down orally over the years, and have become rounded and shaped by this oral tradition. A comparison can be made with the stories, sayings and parables of Jesus as contained within the Gospel of St Mark. Here again, we find the same pattern of separate stories or sayings strung together to form the impression of an overall whole. Yet the sayings and stories often have no real link with what comes before or after. So it is with the *Tao Te Ching*. Wise sayings or oracles were passed down from one person to the next and in the process became perfectly shaped to fulfil the task of capturing and expressing the insight which they contained. These were orally transmitted and then committed to writing later. Gradually, over a period of many decades and centuries, these gathered around the name of Lao Tzu until they were edited somewhere between 350 and 300 BC.

What is interesting is that only sayings and oracles coalesced around Lao Tzu's name. No stories were added. This gives us an important clue as to the nature of the chapters and this I shall want to look at shortly.

Where do these sayings and oracles come from? As indicated above, they arise from the tradition of the shaman oracles. Questions would be posed to the gods by means of divination items such as tortoise shells and ox shoulder bones. These were heated at certain points on them and the cracks which resulted were then read as giving a message. These oracles were no doubt supplemented by sayings from highly renowned shamans. These would have been collected and passed down as being of perennial significance. China is rich in such materials. The *I Ching* is the oldest collection of these types of text – it is much older than anything within the *Tao Te Ching*. There are echoes here and there in the *Tao Te Ching* of *I Ching* sayings, such as in Chapter 53, but the *I Ching* sayings are of a different character. They are very complex. They appear to have no logic to them. They are esoteric in the sense that they seem to defy understanding. As such they represent a divination oracle style which has continued in unbroken form to this day. In the temples of the Chinese around the world, you will find similar types of oracular sayings claiming to be revelations by gods such as Won Tai Sin or the female Buddhist deity, Kuan Yin. These terse sayings, often linking sentences which seem to

make no sense, require the services of a fortune teller or priest to interpret their meaning.

The *Tao Te Ching* is not in that category of text, though it comes close to it at times. In the *Tao Te Ching* we see a development from these terse texts to something much more interesting. For in its chapters we find more developed sayings, and with them come commentaries and expositions of the text. Sometimes, these sayings are more in the nature of proverbs – what my colleague on this book, Jay, describes as 'peasant wisdom'. A good example of this peasant wisdom and commentary style is found in Chapter 44. It opens with a set of direct questions about what is really important in life. The proverb/questions are direct and simple. Then they are commented on in the next four lines and the whole chapter is then summed up in the final commentary section at the end of the chapter.

In the *Tao Te Ching* we have a set of separate chapters which have been strung together. This means that in many cases each chapter is complete in itself. This completeness is what makes the book so powerful. For we are not just given a saying or oracle insight, but we are also given an exposition and commentary which helps us, often through the use of further imagery, to penetrate to the heart of the saying. While some fall into the peasant wisdom category, many can best be described as wisdom sayings – encapsulations of insight and truth refined down the centuries. With each of these also comes the commentary. Thus within one chapter we have not just the teaching or wisdom saying, but also an explanation of the meaning of the saying. That even these explanations are of great antiquity and insight, is what makes the *Tao Te Ching* so exciting.

Take Chapter 1 as an example. It opens with some of the most powerful lines in the entire book – lines which have taxed translators down the ages! The first five lines, from 'The Tao that can be talked about is not the true Tao' down to 'While Heaven, the mother is the creatrix of all things', are the original wisdom saying or oracle. They are beautifully balanced texts in the original Chinese. They pair with each other and have a style which is quite breathtaking in both its terseness (especially the first two lines), and its depth of meaning. Thus the first two lines are two pairs of three characters which perfectly balance and reflect each other. Then the third and fourth lines (in our translation rendered into three lines to capture the depth of meaning) are a pair of sentences with six characters in each, and again, with a balance and symmetry between them which is a delight to behold.

Here is the original set of sayings or wisdom oracles. What comes after that is commentary and exposition. Still written in a beautiful and profound style, they lack within their structure in Chinese the deliberate balance and reflection which is found in the earlier sentences. Looking at the translation which runs from 'Follow the nothingness of the Tao' to the end of the chapter, you will see that their style is very different from the earlier lines and that what is being done is an expansion and elaboration on these earlier lines. This pattern is repeated time and time again throughout the book and convinces us that at heart the *Tao Te Ching* is a collection of core sayings with commentary and expositions. Once this has been appreciated, the relationship between the lines within each chapter is much easier to grasp.

But what is exciting about this is that here is a collection of sayings which differs from all earlier Chinese material. Not only can we encounter the wisdom of the ancient Chinese, but we can also follow their own expositions and explanations. Unlike the *I Ching*, we are not confronted by texts which need yet another book or person to make them accessible. The guide is built into the chapters. This is why the book has become such a favourite in the West, for it not only gives us wisdom sayings, but also helps us delve deeper into the layers of meaning which lie within these sayings.

Another good example is Chapter 8. Here the first four lines (from 'The sage's way . . .' to '. . . is true to Tao') are the wisdom saying. From there to the end, we have a very different kind of text. Here is almost a little sermon on how to behave, loosely based on the earlier text and taking further the water imagery which is used in the first part of the chapter. These latter lines move from slightly ponderous proverb-type preaching into an expansion of the earlier imagery of the first few lines. The chapter is a complete unit in its own right: text, moral and exposition, all in one. It is also worth noting that there is no connection between this chapter and Chapters 7 and 9, other than that they are exploring the nature of the Tao. The imagery does not flow from one to the other. They stand as isolated, single units.

Not all of the chapters exhibit this style of sayings and commentary. Some are simply sayings or wisdom. Others seem to be more rambling commentaries on themes which have arisen before and are now explored a bit further. This is particularly true of the texts from Chapter 71 onwards.

Scattered amongst these chapters are a few which are striking for their directness. This is because they speak in the first person and could be described as almost autobiographical. You feel as if the sage is revealing his innermost soul to you and it is both thrilling and slightly alarming at the same time. Chapter 20 is the best example of this. Here the sage describes himself in contradistinction to the norms of his society. In frank and sharply defined language he says:

Only, you see, I am lazy
And I don't give a damn about fame or money.
I am like a child who cannot bring himself to smile.

What do the people want? Money and things.
And yet I find I have nothing, and I don't care.
I am as unambitious as any fool.

And the people, the people are so busy!
But I have nothing to bother about. I am a bumpkin, a lout.

I am different, I am strange,
I live for the Mother.

Who is this who speaks so powerfully to us? This is not the well-turned saying and commentary of the other chapters. It belongs to a set of chapters which are in a very different tradition from the bulk of the rest of the text. Others which are similar to Chapter 20, to some degree or another, are Chapters 21, 25, 43, 49, 67 and 70. In all of these, the sage speaks in the first person. They all have a different tone from the other texts. The others strive for, or have achieved, a sense of timelessness or of anonymity. In the seven 'I' chapters, this is reversed. The bluntness of some of these chapters reminds one of the bluntness of the Lao Tzu figure whom K'ung encountered. Is it just possible that what we have here is the remains of an original Lao Tzu sayings collection? If so, it would explain why they have remained in the first person while the rest is in the third person when discussing the sage. We shall never know, but it is just possible that what we have here is a glimpse of the personality of Lao Tzu, to whom so much else was later credited, speaking directly to us. If it is not Lao Tzu, then the editor of the *Tao Te Ching* obviously respected this collection of sayings sufficiently not to try and make them fit in with the usual style of the rest of the book. Whoever is the 'I' behind these seven texts, he must have been a person of such significance that his directness and personality have been allowed to come down to us.

Having tried to give some feel for the styles broadly present within the book, I want to turn to its actual editing.

Ssu-ma Ch'ien, in his account of the writing of the book, says that Lao Tzu wrote it in two parts. These are what are known as the Tao section, from Chapter 1 to Chapter 37 and the Te section from Chapter 38 to the end. They are so called because the opening of Chapter 1 talks about the Tao and the opening of Chapter 38 talks about Te. In the earliest version of the text to have survived to this day, a text dating from around 167 BC, the sections are actually round the other way, that is to say the book has become the Te Tao Ching.

While the Te Tao arrangement of this ancient text remains somewhat of an enigma, the recent discovery of this second century BC text does show that the book had achieved its essential form by this time. So we can confidently say that before 167 BC, the *Tao Te* (or *Te Tao*) *Ching* that we largely know today was in existence.

In the year 213 BC an event took place which had a profound impact on many ancient texts. The first Emperor of what we now think of as geographical China – the ruthless Ch'in Shih Huang-ti – ordered all ancient books, with a few exceptions, to be destroyed. It is said that over 460 Confucian scholars were executed for trying to hide the texts of K'ung Fu-tzu. All over China, mass destructions of ancient histories, religious texts and other such volumes took place. The reason for this was simple. Ch'in Shih Huang-ti wanted to practise mind-control. He – or rather his brilliant but brutal Prime Minister, Li Ssu – realized that if all records of other kings and rulers and other wisdom were destroyed, then no one would know that life had ever been or could ever be different from the dictatorship in which they dwelt. It was a frighteningly powerful beginning to the sort of mind-control so beloved by dictators ever since.

In an attempt to save texts from destruction, scholars tried to hide them. Spaces were hollowed in walls, the texts placed in them and then plaster spread over the hollows to hide them. This time-honoured means of saving that which the government sought to destroy was used during the Cultural Revolution when book burning was again the rage. Many books and religious art treasures are still being rediscovered – those who hid them having been either killed or moved thousands of miles away. A similar picture emerges for the book banning of the late third century BC.

Chinese books of that period were not books in the sense that we know them. They were not written on paper and bound into one volume. Nor were they written on scrolls. They were written on strips of bamboo which were then pierced at the top and bottom and tied to the strips on either side. To make up an average chapter of the *Tao Te Ching* you would have had to use roughly three to four such strips. This method of book-making has two characteristics which are important in the understanding of why the text we have today is as it is. First, it is relatively easy to add new sections or parts to the beginning or end of such a 'book'. All you have to do is tie them on to the first or last strip. As we will argue in a moment, this is what happened to the *Tao Te Ching*. Secondly, if the book is not cared for and repaired, then the ties holding the strips will perish quite quickly and you will be left with a collection of strips which it will be rather difficult to reassemble in their right order. It does not appear that the strips were numbered.

In this edition of the *Tao Te Ching* you will find that we have made some changes to the normal format of the text. In part this comes from the awareness of the historical and physical nature of the early texts of the Tao; partly from contemporary Chinese research and commentaries on the text; and partly from our own work and researches in translating it and poeticizing the translation.

Perhaps the most dramatic of these changes, is that we have divided the text into its two main sections – the Tao and the Te – but that we believe that the original Te section ended at Chapter 70. Therefore Chapters 71–81 are treated as a coda. There are three main reasons for this change. First, we noted that from Chapter 71 onwards the quality of the texts declined rapidly from that of the rest of the book. The quality of the Chinese and the repetitive and often superficial nature of these final chapters convinced us that these were of a different order from the rest of the text. With the exception of Chapter 77 and its imagery of the bow, none of these chapters contains an original insight. In almost all cases they simply reiterate themes which have been explored in much greater depth earlier in the book.

The second reason for our new division is based on the actual text of Chapter 70. This is one of the 'I' texts and contains the famous opening lines:

> *My words are really very easy to understand*
> *And be with, and walk in . . . but no one can!*

This chapter mirrors the opening saying contained in Chapter 1. At first it appears to do so by contradicting the sayings in Chapter 1. Is it really saying that the Tao is easy? No, of course it is not, but for a brief moment we are led to think that it is. Gradually, as Chapter 70 unfolds, the unknowability of the Tao is reiterated – but alongside it, we are reminded of the centrality of the Way of Tao – that path which we all can tread if we really come to appreciate what it is. This chapter is one of the most direct and beautiful in the *Tao Te Ching*. Mirroring as it does Chapter 1, we believe that the Te section ended here.

There is a third reason too. There is no question but that the Tao section contains the core of the *Tao Te Ching's* message. The Tao is what the book is about, with the Te playing a supportive role. The Tao section contains 37 chapters. If the existing 81 chapters are all treated as original to the compilation, then the Te section has 44 chapters. We believe this is unlikely. If the eleven final chapters are seen as a later addition, then the Te section has 33 chapters and is thus shorter than the Tao.

In Ssu-ma Ch'ien's account, Lao Tzu is reputed to have written his classic in 5000 characters. The text we have is greater than this. Our conclusion about how the *Tao Te Ching* came to be the text we have today is as follows.

Texts – some dating back to oracles and proverbs from around 1000 BC – were gradually developed through oral telling over centuries into complete units with their own commentaries. These units then gravitated towards one collection, itself a set of more personal units, associated with the name and possibly even the personality of Lao Tzu. At some point around 400 BC, these units were edited into two sections – Tao and Te – which probably ended with our present Chapter 70. The number 7 is a very powerful one in Chinese numerology. All such 'magic' numbers when given the power of 10 keep their power, and indeed sometimes have it enhanced. Thus Chapters 1–70 were the original *Tao Te Ching* or *Lao Tzu* as it was called at that time. There was no deception meant by the editor – himself a person of tremendous insight as the book shows. To use the name of some great figure as author of a text was quite standard. Other texts such as *Chuang Tzu* also show this happening. It was considered to be a perfectly honourable way of commemorating a great figure in history. We shall never know who the actual final compiler of the core *Tao Te Ching* (to Chapter 70) was. He is lost to us in the mists of history. But whoever he was, he was quite exceptional. In bringing together this marvellous collection of texts, he has done us a great service. Thus, by saying that Lao Tzu did not write the *Tao Te Ching*, we are in no way diminishing its unique status and power.

At some point around 300–250 BC, nearly 100 years after the original *Tao Te Ching* of 70 chapters had been completed, the last eleven chapters were added. These chapters, especially 75, 79 and 80, speak of a time of massive and disturbing social change. They record the struggles and rights which small states felt were important, and in Chapter 75 there is an impassioned protest at the domination of the people by an oppressive regime. Chapter 75 contains no statement about the Tao. It is not a philosophical series of observations. It does not mention Te. It is a cry of protest against an unjust, brutal system. Chapter 74, though less passionate, is of a similar ilk – again not containing any of the conventional wisdom found in Chapters 1–70.

In the first seventy chapters, the state is almost always presented as essentially a good thing, more so if it is ruled by a sage or a sagacious ruler. The impression is of a small state, controllable and not overbearing. In the last eleven chapters, (71–81) the picture is of the collapse or threatened collapse of the small state (which is idealized in Chapter 80) and of the fear of the rise of totalitarianism. As such, it seems to reflect the demise, one by one, of the smaller states as the state of Ch'in rose to greater and greater power, culminating in the total victory of Ch'in in 221 BC, the founding of the Ch'in Dynasty and the rule of the aforementioned tyrant, Ch'in Shih Huang-ti. It is for these reasons that we see these later chapters as an additional block of text, added on to the original *Tao Te Ching* some 100 to 150 years after the rest of the book had been compiled from material stretching back to the beginning of the first millennium BC.

The second dramatic change is in the content of a number of the chapters. Following certain current Chinese commentators views on this, we have rearranged a number of lines which appear to have become misplaced. An example, is Chapter 63. The version given here is nearly twice the usual length. This is because we have moved what is usually the second half of Chapter 64 to the beginning of Chapter 63. It fits much better here and introduces the broad theme of the rest of Chapter 63. Chapter 64, in contrast, opens with a set of lines which do not relate to what was its second half – now the opening of Chapter 63. The commentaries suggest that the bamboo strips were broken and then reconnected but with a shift of a block of text. It is easy to see how this could happen: the ties holding the bamboo strips could rot or break and be inexpertly retied.

At various places throughout the text we found sentences misplaced or even repeated, which had no relevance to the chapter they were in. In removing and restoring these lines to their assumed original chapters we have tried to restore the text to its original shape. It seems quite likely that during Ch'in Shih Huang-ti's book-burning phase, many copies of the *Tao Te Ching* were destroyed and those that survived were hidden. When it became possible to retrieve them, they were broken and in the process of reassembling them, some parts were wrongly placed. For those who are interested, the following chapters have been amended in the light of these observations: 15, 20, 21, 29, 32, 34, 39, 42, 43, 55, 63, 64, 67, 76 and 79.

It is now time to move on to explore the message of the *Tao Te Ching* and to look at some aspects of the use of imagery, of cosmology and of socio-political insight which the *Tao Te Ching* delineates as its contribution towards the emergence of Taoism.

We should start with what the Tao is deemed to be. The word *tao* means 'road' or 'pathway'. In Chinese cities it is commonly to be seen on road signs, telling you that this is Shanghai Street (*Tao*) or Nanjing Way (*Tao*). As such it is a word in common use and with a simple functional role. However, since early times, Tao has taken on a much more spiritual and ultimately transcendent meaning. It has done so for exactly the same reasons that have led us in English to speak of the Way of Jesus or the Way of the Buddha. It is the natural use of the image of a path or roadway which leads us to something beyond ourselves. It was also used at an early stage (pre-1000 BC) to mean the course of teachings or the discipline which was necessary to achieve some higher goal. Thus in early texts such as those found in the *Book of History (Shu Ching)*, parts of which date to the Shang dynasty (1523–1028 BC), the Tao is used to describe the right way of going about doing something.

In a text which also includes that other word from the *Tao Te Ching*, namely the Te or Virtue, we read:

> *I see how great is your virtue, how admirable your vast achievements. The specific choice of Heaven rest upon you: you must eventually take the throne of the great ruler. The mind of humanity is restless and likely to fail; its willingness to follow the Way is small. (Part II. Book 2. Ch.II. 14–15)*

This text is addressed by the Emperor to the Mighty Yu. Yu is reputed to have lived around 2000 BC, and here he is being told that in the natural course of events it is likely that he will ascend the imperial throne. The reason is for this that Yu is an exemplary figure and thus best suited to guide the people in living the right way, the Way (Tao) of Heaven.

The word 'Tao' also appears in a slightly different way in other documents within the *Shu Ching*. Here it is combined with the word 'T'ien', which means 'Heaven'. As such it is usually translated as 'the Way of Heaven'. The meaning here seems to be a little bit more cosmic than the Way on its own. The following text comes from the time of King T'ang (*c*1460–61 BC).

> *I have heard the saying: 'He who finds himself teachers, will rule the greatest area; he who says no one is his equal, will fall. He who is willing to ask, becomes greater; he who relies entirely upon himself, will be humbled and made small.' So, he who wishes to be sure of his end, must look to his beginning. There is security for those who observe propriety and disaster for those who are blind and pay no attention. To revere and honour the Way of Heaven is the way to ensure the favour of Heaven for ever. (Part IV. Book 2. Ch. IV. 8–9)*

In this text, doing the right thing is to be in touch with a divinely ordained and guided Way, which is itself a divine reality. It is also interesting to notice how similar to certain parts of the *Tao Te Ching* the first part of the text is. It is a good example of the wisdom saying, around which a commentary formed, which then came to be strung on the string of the *Tao Te Ching*. It is texts such as this which give us the confidence to say that much of the material in the *Tao Te Ching* goes back as far as around 1000 BC.

By the time we reach the editor of the *Tao Te Ching*, about 400 BC, the Tao has become even more profound in its resonances. In part this was due to other figures such as K'ung Fu-tzu. K'ung could be described as one of the earliest Taoists. His writings show the developing ideas of Tao. He forms a very important link between the earlier use of Tao in the *Shu Ching* and the emergence of the truly cosmic Tao in the *Tao Te Ching*. K'ung's writings are fascinating because of the range of uses he illustrates. On occasions, he uses the term Tao in a very limited, rather moralistic and legalistic, way:

> *The Master said: 'Riches and honours are what people want. If these cannot be gained in the right Way [Tao], they should not be kept. Poverty and meanness are what people dislike. If it had been obtained in the right Way [Tao] then I would not try to avoid them.' (The Analects, Book 4:5)*

In Book 16 of *The Analects*, K'ung uses language about the Tao which is almost identical to the *Tao Te Ching*:

K'ung Tzu said: 'When the Way prevails in the world, the rites, music and punitive military expeditions are initiated by the Emperor (Son of Heaven). When the Way does not prevail in the world, they are initiated by the lesser lords . . . When the Way prevails in the world policy is not in the hands of Councillors. When the Way prevails in the world, there is nothing for the ordinary people to argue about.'

This is remarkably close to the themes developed in chapters such as 17 and 18 in the *Tao Te Ching*.

Finally, K'ung comes to speak of the Tao in a way which could almost be Lao Tzu speaking. This statement is credited to him in the opening lines of *The Doctrine of the Mean*:

What Heaven has given is called the law of Nature. To follow this natural way is to follow the Way. To nurture this Way is called learning. The Way must not be left, even for a moment. If it could be left, then it would not be the Way.

While K'ung comes close to some of the ideas of the Tao as expressed in the *Tao Te Ching*, ultimately the Tao is more a part of a given moral code, albeit with heavenly sanction. In the end the Confucians turned more to the Te – Virtue – than to the Tao as a way of keeping the world on the right lines.

This brings us to the very distinctive use of the Tao within the *Tao Te Ching*. In essence, the *Tao Te Ching* lays out a cosmological view of the universe wherein the Tao is not just the path of heaven; it is not just the purpose of heaven; is not even the origin of all life in the universe; it is the origin of the Origin. Chapter 42:

The Tao
gives birth to the One;
The One
gives birth to the two;
The Two
give birth to the three;
The Three give birth to every living thing.
All things are held in yin, and carry yang:
And they are held together in the Ch'i
of teeming energy.

The Tao begets the One – the Origin. From this, according to later classical Chinese cosmology, come the twin opposite forces of yin and yang. From these come the three legs of the tripod as they are known – Heaven, Earth and humanity. From these flow all creativity – all species, land, waters and civilization. In this beautifully succinct cosmological creed, the Tao is beyond even the Origin. It is the source of the Origin. Other verses, such as Chapter 4, convey this same sense of the absoluteness of the Tao, and of course the famous opening chapter does so in a more mysterious way. But Chapter 42 is the boldest and clearest statement, taking the notion of the Tao to its ultimate extent – as the origin of even the Origin.

Elsewhere in the text, we come across a variety of meanings for the Tao. In many places it is much more the Way of Nature, or the Natural Way. These texts, exemplifying what Jay calls the 'water theme' in the book, contain a lesser notion of the Tao. It is the means or insight which comes from knowing one's place within the greater world of the forces of nature. Chapter 8 is an example of such a text. Similarly, the old *Shu Ching* 'Way of Heaven' appears in some chapters, such as Chapter 9. I would argue that these texts are quite early ones, dating from the period from about 1000 to 600 BC. They do not have the same degree of elevation of the Tao as Chapters 1 and 42, texts which were formed around 600 – 400 BC, display.

In the end, the variety of understandings of the Tao does not matter because they work together to give us a rounded picture of its height, depth and breadth. This is the skill of the unknown editor. He wove a series of texts together in such a way that the variety enhances our appreciation of the Tao rather than diminishes it. We experience it as both the origin of the Origin and as present in all, as the path that is to be followed, that can be walked now, and as that which ultimately is beyond following or knowledge, as the right way and as the way which will be scorned.

In achieving this understanding, the role of the sage is vital. The sage is, like the Tao, many things. He is the wise and astute ruler. He is the person who lets things go by. He is the recluse.

He is the lynchpin of a society. But more than this, he is both a guide and the model of the Way. As such he speaks to us directly and individually – which is one of the abiding strengths of the *Tao Te Ching*. He is a contemporary figure in both the style of what he says and the content. Man-Ho Kwok and I translated the *Tao Te Ching* during the run-up to the Gulf War of 1991 and during the War itself. Constantly we found ourselves saying things like: 'We should send this chapter to President Bush/Saddam Hussein' or 'If only people had listened to the sage in the years before the invasion of Kuwait, what a difference that would have made.' The texts seemed as relevant during that crisis as they must have seemed in their own time.

At a more personal level, the sage is a pilgrim guide. He shows a path which makes sense and which relocates us in the Way. This is a quite extraordinary role that he plays. It is made possible by those 'I' chapters which turn what could otherwise have been a rather remote, worldly wise figure into a contemporary one. In just the same way as the Psalms contain both the grand and the personally tragic, the powerful and the emotionally honest, so the *Tao Te Ching* contains the austere and the intimate, and in doing so, like the Psalms, is both contemporary and timeless.

The nature of the path of the sage is captured in a few key phrases within the text. In essence it is about being centred, being rooted within that which is of nature, the natural Tao. When someone is thus centred, all becomes possible, but also all falls into place. This leads to the notion of *wu-wei*, or non-action.

As the end of Chapter 5 says: 'There are too many laws, when all you have to do is to hold on to the centre.' The concept is that at the heart of all things is the ultimate Tao, origin of origins and effective through all things. All that leads to or encourages unity is thus seen as being of the Tao. Chapter 37 expresses this:

And if parts still want to separate,
the true leader will use
> *the centrifugal weight*
of this original
>> *unnameable Oneness.*

It is the Tao that holds all things together, but it does this at its best through the silent but effective working of the sagacious ruler. The sage rules in such a way that no one knows the rules. Chapter 3 says:

The sage always make sure
that the people don't know what he's done,
so they never want to take control –
and they are never driven by ambition.

He keeps them in truth like this
> *acting invisibly.*

In this, the sage mirrors the very nature of the Tao itself. Chapter 10 describes the Tao in action:

It gives without holding on to what it's made,
It gives everything essence without reward,
It knows, without flaunting it,
It is serene, beyond desiring

– and this is its Virtue and its Source.

How does the Tao work? The book tells us that the Tao and the sage act through lack of action. This is but one of the different ways the term *wu-wei* has been translated. It is a complex idea, which is not adequately captured by the term non-action, as this is, in English, a negative statement. Rather one should picture *wu-wei* as being active nothingness – the hollow at the centre which is described in Chapter 11. It is also the concept of doing for no reward – of being beyond any personal interest in anything. This lack of desire or ambition, this wish not to benefit from any undertaking, is another dimension of the *wu-wei* idea. It is only really through encountering the term and its different nuances within the text that an adequate grasp of the depths of this idea can be gained. Do not settle for one phrase alone – for that will inevitably be too shallow a meaning.

The image of the Tao as penetrating and getting into the very heart of issues is also strong within the text. It comes as part of the water imagery which Jay will comment on later in this introduction. The idea that just as water can penetrate even the toughest rock and crack it open or wear it down, so the Tao operates in the world. Chapter 43 is a good example of this understanding of the Tao. It is this sense of the Tao reaching within all things and by its mere existence cracking open or opening up all things, which gives the *Tao Te Ching* such a profound sense of insight. We learn that nothing is outside or closed to the Tao and as such we know that if we look within anything, not least ourselves, the Tao is there, silently, doing nothing, and wishing intensely to do nothing other than be. And in that be-ing lies its ultimateness and its immanence.

I want now to turn, briefly, to some of the issues which always arise when doing a translation. In this work, Man-Ho Kwok and I produced a rough and detailed translation in which we would often use three or four terms or phrases to try and capture the essence of what one or two Chinese characters expressed far better. From this, Jay then worked on the poetic translation. As a result, in certain chapters, Jay has added an extra line within which he has captured an additional meaning of a word or phrase given in the line above. As it is always impossible to translate direct from one language to another, and this is doubly so when dealing with a spiritual and philosophical text as profound as the *Tao Te Ching*, we hope that readers will enjoy this assistance with the nuances and forgive the licence of the odd extra line.

In certain other places, there came another problem. That is the assumed knowledge which would underlie a given image. Take for instance Chapter 38. The final seven verses assume familiarity with an ancient Chinese proverb and story. The proverb is 'Don't throw away the water just because it has dust on it', with the implication that outward appearances may not do justice to the depths and quality within.

There is also a fine old story told of one of the geomancer masters. This master had been out to look at a site chosen for a very illustrious grave. He had made all the observations and found it to be in a very auspicious place. However, it took three days of walking to get to the remote spot and as he headed home, he ran out of water. Twenty-four hours later he was des-

perate. Then in the distance he saw a woman and her three sons working in the fields. Hurrying towards them he asked for some water, explaining that he had not drunk for a full day. The woman poured some water from her gourd into a bowl. Then, to the feng shui master's great annoyance, she sprinkled chaff on top of the water. He tried to gulp down the water, but found the chaff kept getting in the way, thus slowing his drinking. More and more annoyed, he deliberately gave the woman some bad feng shui advice about where to have her house, and left, feeling very disgruntled.

Five years later he passed that way again. He was amazed to be greeted with thanks by the woman. She invited him into her new house, which was very comfortable. She told him of the remarkable success of her sons, who were all doing well. The feng shui master asked how this could possibly be, given that he had directed her to build the house in a site which should have brought very bad fortune. When the woman asked why he had been so cruel, he reminded her about soiling his water with chaff.

'Didn't you realize?' laughed the woman, 'it was a hot day, you had travelled a long way, and I knew you were exhausted. You were so thirsty that you would have swallowed the water in one go and the shock of the cold water would have been too much for you. You had to blow on the water to clear the chaff each time you took a mouthful and so you drank it more slowly. I was trying to protect you.'

The feng shui master realized his own foolishness and saw now why the gods of the area had rewarded the woman, despite his having given her bad advice.

Any well-read Chinese, coming to these lines, would know of the proverb and probably of the story. So how does one convey this in a translation to those for whom both story and proverb are unknown? Well, one way is by putting it in the introduction, but then we know that most people skip introductions! Thus Jay has tried in his translation to convey some sense of this image but without doing too much by way of expanding the text. 'Blow away the dust, now come to the living water.'

Another problem is the translation of words which seem to have an exact meaning but which actually carry a wider sense than the precise translation. A very common word in the *Tao Te Ching* is *wan*. This strictly means ten thousand but it is used also to describe all life on earth, which according to ancient Chinese thinking, consisted of 10,000 species. It is often given in translations as either 'ten thousand' or as 'myriad' – which means ten thousand but also has the connotation of a greater number than that. We have found these terms confusing to people. Given that the Chinese is trying to express that all things come from the Tao, we have used phrases such as 'Life, all life' (Chapter 2) or 'every living thing' (Chapter 39).

There are just a few other pointers which readers unfamiliar with Chinese life and thought might find helpful. In Chapter 10 'souls' are mentioned. According to Chinese belief, everyone has a plurality of souls. The numbers differ according to which texts or sects you follow. However, there are normally seen to be either two or three. This plurality of souls assists the Chinese in being able to believe that the soul of the deceased ancestor watches over the family, at the same time as being judged in heaven and punished prior to rebirth. Hence the term 'souls' in Chapter 10. In Chapter 12 we have the five colours, the five notes and the five tastes. Five is a very powerful number in Chinese belief, being the five points of the compass (all the usual ones plus the Centre) which is in itself a picture of the totality of existence. Hence, the use of the number five in association with colours, notes and tastes means we are dealing with the total range of such items.

In Chapter 15, Jay has used the word 'sorcerers'. The idea of a sorcerer in ancient Chinese thought was of someone of evil intent. This is not meant here. It is an instance of using a term from English which will convey a clear idea of a resourceful, magical person, but we want to make clear that it is not a direct translation of the Chinese term, which would better be described as 'shaman'.

In giving a few more notes of this kind, we have tried to prepare the reader for the fact that this text arose within an ancient culture where much which was commonplace to them, is odd or unknown to us. Likewise, there are terms which make sense to us, but which would alarm a traditional Chinese reader! Jay has sought at various times to provide, through an additional line, some sense or feeling for the complexity of issues and cross-cultural differences which make translation such a challenging and occasionally rewarding task. We hope that purists will excuse the additional lines or amplifications, in the pursuit of a clearer understanding of the essential insights and wisdom of this most extraordinary book.

The *Tao Te Ching* has influenced Chinese thought for over two thousand years. Within it, for the very first time, the diversity and depth of the concept of Tao, so fundamental to both philosophical and 'religious' Taoism, appeared.

In the writings of other forerunners of the Taoist movement, such as Chuang Tzu, we see these ideas much more systematically and amusingly developed. The *Tao Te Ching* remains aloof from the other Taoist texts. It may be that there once was a Lao Tzu, some of whose sayings are encapsulated within the existing book. As I have said, we would argue that from Chapter 71 onwards we are dealing with much later texts, not part of the original book. What remains without question is that whoever it was who edited the collection of wisdom sayings and teachings, some time in the fifth to fourth centuries BC, was a genius. Although unknown to us, his work continues to speak to us and to challenge us to re-examine our thoughts and ways. It is perhaps not without significance that the *Tao Te Ching* is one of the few religious texts which can be read and enjoyed by people of many different faiths as well as by those of no specific faith. It has no creator God. It has no deities. It has no spirits or religious dogmas. What it has is the notion of the Way – a Way which we each need to make our own, but which flows through time and cultures, just as the river, so often pictured in the text, flows naturally down to the sea, bringing everything with it.

Martin Palmer

My approach overall in translating this classic text has been very much of a late twentieth century poet. There are several reasons for this. Reading other translations of the *Tao* before I actually began work, what struck me was an 'Anglo-Chinese' style I wanted to move away from as I felt this had been exhausted. To attempt to create yet another translation in English sounding like Chinese would have been merely repetitive.

Conversations with both Peter (Man-Ho Kwok) and Martin Palmer have been crucial to this process – and as Martin himself said, this text is not one that would have been treated like a sacred cow, sacred as it is: it would have been discussed and argued over as anecdotes about the meeting of sages illustrate.

So what was to be our approach? What we wanted to do was to try and get as close to the spirit of the original as possible – to get under the layers of repetitive 'translationese' and give it a fresh exposition. Like many others, I'd been inspired by Ezra Pound's translations, not only of Chinese poems, but of Provençal and Anglo-Saxon as well, because what he had achieved by freeing up the literal was an instilling of atmosphere and spirit. You can *feel* the poems, and what they're saying. Another connection for me here, as a poet writing after him, has to do with the techniques of Modernism he was so central in initiating, and his influence on my own work is there, although the tone and music are different. Pound himself went deeper and deeper into Chinese, and having developed the technique of the 'stepped line', his

later Cantos increasingly use ideograms, so that the shape of the words on the page becomes a part of the poetry's meaning.

I wanted to use these techniques as I've developed them myself, and because given the form and spirit of the original – hanging as it did in vertical strips – it seemed to me actually to come closest to it. And that was exciting.

My other main intention right from the beginning was to communicate beyond technique, and what was in my mind was Rimbaud's dictum 'Il faut etre absolument moderne' (one must be absolutely modern), and there may be those of you reading this that don't care at all about these technical issues, and that's fine! What matters, of course, is the substance, the content and the essence – and that the technique liberates this for us now.

But dwelling on it is not merely technical. It says something about what the original itself is, and this is why I wanted to share our method. It brings what we are working with into closer and clearer focus.

What is obvious from the original, as Martin has pointed out, is two basic styles we referred to as 'the cryptic' and 'the commentary'. The first is essentially elliptical, terse and poetic – the second more explanatory and prosaic. I've generally delineated the first, which is usually mystical as well, by using stepped lines. This is where the line breaks, and literally 'steps' downwards, giving the impression of suspension, of hanging in space. The second I've indicated with longer lines that are set in lower case at the beginnings of those lines. There are exceptions, as later chapters themselves become more prosey, which I'll comment on.

Again, what interested me from the beginning was the tone and music of the original, and I wanted to know as much about this as possible. It struck me that 'the cryptic' and 'the commentary' were integral to each other – like Heaven and Earth – and I felt also that the energies of yin and yang were there, where the yang would be more terse and crystalline, and the yin more lyrical and fluid. The yin, the feminine, is absolutely essential to understanding the Tao, and is implied throughout – as we will see.

Peter and Martin subsequently marked up each chapter of the literals they made, indicating three, four or five character sentences and commenting on rhythm and pattern or its absence, and occasionally rhyme as well. This was invaluable. It gave me a key, in some sense, to divining each chapter – listening into the ground of its language, getting its feeling as I faced each blank sheet of my own paper.

I want to say a little about ancient and modern now from this end, and in this context.

I have retained throughout traditional terms and names like 'the sage' and 'the Emperor' rather than using terms like 'wise person' or even 'President' (these can be implied). The only other translation that spoke to me personally was Stephen Mitchell's, and in it he bravely tries to make the sage into a woman as well. But much as I sympathize with this, I don't think it really works. The sage *is* masculine, but what he represents as a channel, and through his particular sensitivity as well as pragmatism, is also the feminine. I think this is important. Likewise, the term 'Emperor', as well as being literal, has so many implications not only on the inner as a symbol of masculinity, but more poignantly in the relationship to the imperialism that followed the *Tao* in China, contrary to all its wisdom and warnings, and not only, of course, in China but in Europe and latterly America and the Third World as well. The issue remains.

I have also retained traditional references and analogies (for instance, to the sacrificial bowl in Chapter 9) as they are unerringly precise as well as redolent with Chinese flavour as images. In other translations they have sometimes been glossed over: to me they are vital concrete moments in a text that repeatedly points to the inadequacy of all language, and enacts its mystery through that recognition, right from the opening phrase. I have also – and partly as a result of this – deliberately included the phonetic representation of Chinese words like *Te* (Virtue), *ch'i* (energy), *ch'ang* (nurturing) and *wu-wei* (doing without doing) in the poems I've made, because those concepts are vital and because, as well as echoing at moments the actual sound of the original, they go

beyond what we have partially understood in the West as regards Tao and yin and yang: and they challenge *our* conceptualizations and our absorption of them. This was something I found myself becoming increasingly aware of as the work affected me and entered into me.

The other main point here has to do with authorship, as Martin has already described. Finding that Lao Tzu, like Homer, was almost certainly a title of collective authorship was liberating. What it left me facing was an anthology in which (by definition) more than one voice is present, so I could approach each chapter like a hand coming fresh to its subject. It also gave me breathing space to work on the inclusion of different styles and tones of voice within the whole – and to attempt to bring ancient and modern together not only through the formal, but also the lyrical and the colloquial as well. On this level, I have not only varied tones within a particular poem, but also, occasionally, taken liberties as they suggested themselves, following Peter and Martin's work on the placing of certain groups of lines in certain chapters: so, for instance, Chapter 63 is a new one in this respect, pitched from the point of view of a layman, a man amongst the people. My own feeling is that the text moves increasingly in the direction of 'the people', and that this is what the coda is really about; so I have at moments echoed what a contemporary Taoist might feel, and how we ourselves would speak in that position, seeing things that way.

This also comes out of my conviction as to how much the Tao has to offer us now, not only spiritually, but politically and ecologically as well at this time. Taoism is as radical now as it was then, long before the name 'Taoism' even came into being. And this, like the Gospels, is its timelessness – a timelessness also ironically connected with the fact that we haven't yet got the point, but also (as I will always remember) in terms of what Peter said to me in his restaurant over the table about what it means for Chinese people today 'to undertake the Tao in their hearts'.

At the same time, the original remains: and I have done my best to allow a modern idiom to express it rather than override it – as at moments it could so easily do. The clue lies in contemplating the original, which is always – by its nature – more subtle and inexhaustible. . . like the Tao itself.

Finally, then, one or two more things about structure and form.

One of the chief Western misrepresentations of the Tao and Taoism has to do with its passivity. It includes the passive, and the pacifist, for sure – and memorably so – but it is also dynamic and active, and not merely 'yang' in this sense. Taoism is grounded in the processes and energies of the natural world, as its roots in shamanism further emphasize; and the text is not – or so I feel – a static field of expression. Likewise the yin-yang relationship, far from being an imagistic cliché is a dynamic one in its rising and falling, closer in essence to the spirit of Alchemy (Sol and Luna) than to misty black and white photography. It is fiery as well as watery, though the significant elements in the text are largely water and earth rather than fire and air. The yin, as the opening lines of Chapter 28 counsel, is predominant: hardness and rigidity are constantly countered by softness, apparent weakness and fluidity. The *Tao Te Ching* is about flowing with – with all its implications as regards our personal wills and intentions; and at the heart of this is the paradox of *wu-wei*, surely the most challenging concept for us now, and precisely because it doesn't mean just sitting about doing nothing. It means 'being', it means being receptive, and it means going beyond our egos in what we do and how we do what we do: and this is what the sage personifies, exemplifies and above all, embodies.

His is 'the way of water': and as I've said, it is the feminine, emphasized as it is in the references to the Mother. The Mother is key – as she is in the West, as Sophia (literally 'Mother of Wisdom'). Her presence is immanent and in everything, just as the Tao, which is beyond gender, is 'in every thing' (or 'the ten thousand things', as they've often been translated). Flow, and flowingness, are basic then – and this is how I've tried to represent the poems on paper, not only individually, but together as they follow on.

What I came to, in working on the text, was to structure the whole thing as a river – from source to delta; so that each poem is an instance of river: sometimes a vista of water, sometimes water flowing or bubbling round a rock or between two rocks. And rivers are like this. They are non-linear, as the text itself is. That doesn't mean they are non-sequential or inconsequential – far from it. But they are not logical – not 'left brain', and the *Tao* at every stage exhibits this kind of intuition both in its meaning and in its music.

What I wanted to do was to echo that, not only in its overall shape, but in the spontaneity of certain moments (and spontaneity was very much a part of this translation for me as it unfolded). The poems are designed to breathe and to happen in this way, and as well as creating organic patterns through them, and allowing them to be like that, I've also used ideogrammatic patterning in some spreads throughout the text so that they shape their meaning on the page as I've said – and as a gesture of the Tao's abundant and constant creativity as I understand it.

The Tao is like a river, but it is also like a mountain in its ascending and descending curve, from its apex (we felt) in Chapter 54. Thereafter the original text does become increasingly more prosaic, but rather than just seeing it as a 'falling off', which in one sense it is, it can also be seen as a coming to ground; not only of delta but also of reality – a reality the coda section we have made abruptly points to in its jarring echoes of exploitation and misuse of power. Its tone seems almost tragic, just as earlier chapters, with hindsight, can be seen to be prophetic. The days of the smaller states were about to be over – and now perhaps they will come again, and not even because we necessarily want them to, but because they have to. We have to learn, now more than ever, what it means to live together.

There is a newness that the Tao points to like a dawn, and like a recognition of what has always been here. This freshness is poetry, and so I have not used prose. Apart from being a poet – if it's possible to say this – I see the essence of the Tao as poetic, with all that that implies, and all we still have to learn – to really be here, and to let go.

Jay Ramsay

TAO

道

老子道德 上篇

一章

道可道，非常道。名可名，非常名。

「無」名天地之始；「有」名萬物之母。

故常無，欲以觀其妙；常有，欲以觀其徼。

此兩者同出而異名，同謂之玄。玄之又玄，眾妙之門。

The Tao that can be talked about is not the true Tao.

The name that can be named
is not the eternal Name.

Everything in the universe comes out of Nothing.

Nothing – the nameless
is the beginning;
While Heaven, the mother
is the creatrix of all things.

Follow the nothingness of the Tao,
and you can be like it, not needing anything,
seeing the wonder and the root of everything.

And even if you cannot grasp this nothingness,
you can still see something of the Tao in everything.

These two are the same
only called by different names

– and both are mysterious and wonderful.

All mysteries are Tao, and Heaven is their mother:
She is the gateway and the womb-door.

Chapter two

Beauty and mercy are only recognized by people
Because they know the opposite, which is ugly and mean.

If the people think they know goodness
Then all they really know is what evil is like!

Nothing, and Heaven
                    share the same root –
Difficulty and ease are a part of all work.

The long and the short are in your hands,
Above and below exist because they each do,
What you want and what you say should be the same . . .
Neither future nor past can exist alone.

The sage has no attachment to anything,
and he therefore does what is right without speaking
by simply being
                    in the Tao.

是以聖人處無為之事，行不言之教。萬物作焉而不辭，生而不有，為

而不恃，功成而弗居。夫唯弗居，是以不去。

二章

天下皆知美之為美，斯惡己；皆知善之為善，斯不善己。

故有無相生，難易相成，長短相較，高下相傾，音聲相和，前後相隨。

Life, all life
      began without words.

Life is made – and no one owns it.

The Tao is neither selfish nor proud.

The Tao is generous and graceful in what it does
Without ever claiming any merit

And the sage's greatness lies
in taking no credit.

三章

不尚賢，使民不爭。不貴難得之貨，使民不為盜。不見可欲，使民心不亂。

是以聖人之治：虛其心，實其腹，強其骨，弱其志，常使民無知無欲。

使夫知者不敢為也。為無為，則無不治。

Chapter three

If the sage refuses to be proud
Then people won't compete for his attention:

If the sage does not buy treasures
Then the people won't want to steal them:

If the sage governs with vision
Then his people will not go wrong.

So in his wisdom, he restrains himself:

– by not being greedy for food

– by not dominating the State

– by keeping himself healthy and fit.

The sage always makes sure
that the people don't know what he's done,
so they never want to be in control –
and are never driven by ambition.

He keeps them in truth like this
                              acting invisibly.

You see, if there is nothing to fight for
then there is nothing that can break the flow.

Chapter four

The Tao
>   pours out everything into life –
It is a cornucopia
>   that never runs dry.

It is the deep source of everything –
>   it is nothing, and yet in everything.

It smooths round sharpness
and untangles the knots.

It glows like the lamp
that draws the moth . . .

Tao exists, Tao *is*
but where It came from I do not know.

It has been shaping things
>   from before the First Being,
>   from the before the Beginning of Time.

四章

道沖而用之或不盈。淵兮似萬物之宗。挫其銳，解其紛，和其光，同其塵。湛兮似或存。吾不知誰之子。象帝之先。

動

而愈出。

五章

天地不仁,以萬物為芻狗。聖人不仁,以百姓為芻狗。天地之間,其猶橐籥乎!虛而不屈,動而愈出。

Chapter five

Heaven and earth
                    are not like humans.

The Tao does not act like a human.

They don't expect to be thanked
for making life,
so they view it without expectation.

Heaven and earth are like a pair of bellows:
they are empty, and yet they can never be exhausted.

Work them, and they produce more and more

– there's too much talking, it's really better to stay quiet.

There are too many laws, when all you have to do
                    is to hold on to the centre.

Chapter six

The Tao
> is the breath that never dies.

It is a Mother to All Creation.

It is the root and ground of every soul

– the fountain of Heaven and Earth, laid open.

> Endless source, endless river
> River of no shape, river of no water
> Drifting invisibly from place to place

. . . it never ends
> and it never fails.

谷神不死，是謂玄牝。玄牝之門，是謂天地根。緜緜若存，用之不勤。

六章

Chapter seven

Heaven and earth
                    are enduring.

The universe can live for ever,
because it does not live for itself.

And so both last – outliving themselves.

The sage guides his people
by putting himself last.

Desiring nothing for himself,
he knows how to channel desires.

And is it not because he wants nothing
that he is able to achieve everything?

七章

天長地久。天地所以長且久者，以其不自生，故能長生。是以聖人後其身先，外其身而身存。非以其無私邪？故能成其私。

八章

上善若水。水善利萬物而不爭，處眾人之所惡，故幾於道。居善地，心善淵。與善仁。言善信。正善治。事善能。動善時。夫唯不爭，故無尤。

40

Chapter eight

The sage's way,

Tao

is the way of water.

There must be water for life to be,
and it can flow wherever.

And water, being true to being water
is true
to Tao.

Those on the Way of Tao, like water
need to accept where they find themselves;
and that may often be where water goes
to the lowest places, and that is right.

Like a lake
the heart must be calm and quiet
having great depth beneath it.

The sage rules with compassion,
and his word needs to be trusted.

The sage needs to know like water
how to flow around the blocks
and how to find the way through without violence.

Like water, the sage should wait
for the moment to ripen and be right:

water, you know, never fights

it flows around
without harm.

Chapter nine

Hold yourself back from filling yourself up,
or you'll tip off your stand.

You can hammer a blade until it's razor-sharp –
and in seconds, it can blunt.

You may amass gold and jade in plenty
but then the more you have, the less safety . . .

Are you strutting your wealth like a peacock?
Then you've set yourself up to be shot.
You bring about your own disaster
Because you've got too much.

Let go, when your work is done:

That is the Way of Heaven.

九章

持而盈之，不如其已。揣而梲之，不可長保。金玉滿堂，莫之能守。富貴而驕，自遺其咎。功遂身退，天之道。

十章

載營魄抱一，能無離乎！專氣致柔，能嬰兒乎！滌除玄覽，能無疵乎！愛民治國，能無知乎！天門開闔，能為雌乎！明白四達，能無為乎！生之畜之。生而不有，為而不恃，長而不宰，是謂玄德。

Chapter ten

Can you nurture your souls by holding them
in unity with the One?

Can you focus your *ch'i* – your energy
and become as supple, as yielding as a baby?

Can you clear your mind of all its dross
without throwing out the Tao with it?

Can you do it without self-interest
so you shine like a diamond?

Can you love the people of your nation
without being pulled into action?

Can you turn yourself around
and let Her rise up over you?

The world spans out in four directions –
and can you be as embracing?

Birthing, nurturing and sustaining:
the Tao does this unceasingly . . .

It gives without holding on to what it's made,

It gives everything essence, without reward

It knows, without flaunting it

It is serene, beyond desiring

– and this is its Virtue and its Source.

Chapter eleven

Thirty spokes on a cartwheel

Go towards the hub that is the centre

– but look, there is nothing at the centre
and that is precisely why it works!

If you mould a cup   you have to make a hollow:
it is the emptiness within it that makes it useful.

In a house or room   it is the empty spaces
– the doors, the windows – that make it useable.

They all use what they are made of
to do what they do,

but without their nothingness they would be nothing.

十一章

三十輻共一轂，當其無有，車之用。埏埴以為器，當其無有，器之用。鑿戶牖以為室，當其無有，室之用。故有之以為利，無之以為用。

Chapter twelve

五色令人目盲。五音令人耳聾。五味令人口爽。馳騁畋獵令人心發狂。難得之貨令人行妨。是以聖人為腹不為目。故去彼取此。

十二章

The five colours

         blind the eye –

The five notes

         deafen the ear . . .

The five tastes

         deaden the mouth:

Riding the chase on horseback over the fields
drives you crazy when you overdo it;

And wanting what's precious
you do what distorts your being.

The sage knows this in his gut,
And is guided

         by his instinct

and not by what his eyes want.

十三章

寵辱若驚，貴大患若身。何謂寵辱若驚？寵為下，得之若驚，失之若驚，是謂寵辱若驚。何謂貴大患若身？吾所以有大患者，為吾有身，及吾無身，吾有何患？

故貴以身為天下若可寄天下。愛以身為天下，若可託天下。

Chapter thirteen

Most people fret about themselves and their status,
but you don't have to do this.

What is success and what is failure?

If you have prestige and favour,
all you worry about is that it'll get taken away.
And if you have a lowly place,
you are still basically afraid.
So both, at the root, make for fear.

What does it mean that success is a problem?

It means people are too bound up in themselves.
If they weren't so self-obsessed
they'd have no need to be worried.

If you can put yourself aside –
then you can do things for the whole of the world.
And if you love the world, like this
then you are ready to serve it.

Chapter fourteen

When you gaze at something

                                    but see – nothing;

When you listen for a sound

                                    but cannot hear it;

When you try to grasp it

                                    and find it has no substance

– then these three things
That go beyond your mind
Are moulded together in the One.

Its surface doesn't shine, but nor is its base dull.

Given this, it is only knowable as no-thing.

Confront it – it has no head;

Come behind it, and it has no tail . . .

If people could follow the ancient way,
then they would be masters of the moment.

And if you know this way
then you have seen the timeless way of the Tao.

十四章

視之不見，名曰夷。聽之不聞，名曰希。搏之不得，名曰微。此三者不可詰，故混而為一。

其上不皦，其下不昧。繩繩不可名，復歸於無物。是謂無狀之狀，無物之象。是謂惚恍。迎之不見其首，隨之不見其後。執古之道，以御今之有。能知古始，是謂道紀。

53

十五章

古之善為士者，微妙玄通，深不可識。夫唯不可識，故強為之容。

豫兮若冬涉川，猶兮若畏四鄰。儼兮其若客。渙兮若水之將釋，敦兮其若

樸。曠兮其若谷。混兮其若濁。

孰能濁以？靜之徐清。孰能安以久？動之徐生。

保此道者，不欲盈。夫唯不盈，故能蔽不新成。

Chapter fifteen

In ancient times, the leaders were as subtle as sorcerers.

No one knew what they were about to do.

How can we describe them to you?

They were like soldiers about to cross a cold river,
hesitant, watchful and uncertain.

They were cautious like people who know
there is danger.

They were over-polite, like practised guests.

They gave way like ice, melting

    They were simple like uncarved wood

  They were empty like deserted valleys

They were muddy like unreflecting water.

The mud will settle, and it is hard to wait for it.
But if you can, then you can act.

If you follow the Tao without pretension
            you will never burn yourself out.

Chapter sixteen

The sage rules from the purest motives
Relying wholly on quiet and inner peace.

He watches the seasons rise and fall
And if he knows how things grow, he knows
They are fed by their roots

And they return to their roots;
To grow and flower and flow.

Every thing must have its roots,
and the tendrils work quietly underground.
This quiet feeding is the Way of Nature.

If you understand *ch'ang* – this principle of nurturing,
you can understand everything.
Not understanding it will lead you to disaster.

If a sage knows this, he can rule
And he will do so with patience and justice.

Any man can become wise in this
And he can walk the Way of Heaven

And if you walk that way
You will be royal in the mastery

Life can end in pain –
But if you live like this,
                    under the Tao

You will fill your days with breath.

十六章

致虚極。守靜篤。萬物竝作，吾以觀復。
夫物芸芸，各復歸其根。歸根曰靜，是謂復命。復命曰常。知常
曰明。不知常妄作凶。知常容。容乃公。公乃王。王乃天。天乃道。道乃久。
沒身不殆。

Chapter seventeen

The highest form of government
Is what people hardly even realize is there.

Next is that of the sage
Who is seen, and loved, and respected.

Next down is the dictatorship
That thrives on oppression and terror –

And the last is that of those who lie
And end up despised and rejected.

The sage says little –

and does not tie the people down;

And the people stay happy
Believing that what happens

happens, naturally.

十七章

大上，下知有之；其次親而譽之；其次畏之；其次侮之。

信不足焉。有不信焉。悠兮其貴言！功成事遂，百姓皆謂我自然。

Chapter eighteen

十八章

大道廢，有仁義。慧智出，有大偽。六親不和，有孝慈。國家昏亂，有忠臣。

When the Great Tao is lost sight of –
Then people have to try to be kind and gentle.

They try to compensate by being clever
But this only breeds hypocrisy and sleight-of-hand.

When families fall out
relationships sour into useless formality.

When the nation is misled and in chaos
ministers mouth empty promises.

Chapter nineteen

If the sage could abandon his wisdom and skill,
Then everyone would be a hundred times better off.

If the sage could let go   of holding the scales,
Then everyone would flow in the web of harmony . . .

And if the sage can give up looking to gain,
Then there will be no theft or exploitation.

Now while these three things are important
they are not enough:

The people *themselves* need to learn simplicity.

They shouldn't need to know more than they do,
And should have as few things as possible.

十九章

絕聖棄智，民利百倍。絕仁棄義，民復孝慈。絕巧棄利，盜賊無有。

此三者以為文不足。

故令有所屬，見素抱樸，少私寡欲。

Chapter twenty

Listen, give up trying to be so learned
And things will be a lot easier.

Is there really any difference between a yes
And a no said insincerely?

Is there really much of a difference
Between being angry and pretending not to be?

What the people are afraid of I also need to fear.

And what do most people do? They go
looking for a good time.

They go looking for fool's gold
and auspicious signs.

Only, you see, I am lazy
And I don't give a damn about fame or money.
I am like a child who cannot bring himself to smile.

若無所歸。

眾人皆有餘,而我獨若遺。我愚人之心也哉!沌沌兮!

俗人昭昭,我獨若昏。

俗人察察,我獨悶悶。澹兮其若海,飂兮若無止。

眾人皆有以,我獨頑似鄙。我獨異於人,而貴食母。

What do the people want? Money and things.
And yet I find I have nothing, and I don't care.
I am as unambitious as any fool.

Most people seem to be bright and sharp
And how do I feel? Like a blunted sword.

The people, the people are like waves of sea
And I am drifting between them wherever they are blown.

And the people, the people are so busy!
But I have nothing to bother about. I am a bumpkin, a lout.

I am different, I am strange.
I live for the Mother.

二十章

絕學無憂。唯之與阿,相去幾何?善之与惡,相去若何,人之所畏,

不可不畏。荒兮其未央哉

衆人熙熙,如享太牢,如春登臺。我獨泊兮其未兆。如嬰兒之未孩。儽儽

二十一章

孔德之容，惟道是從。道之為物，惟恍惟惚。惚兮恍兮，其中有象。恍兮惚兮，其中有物。窈兮冥兮，其中有精。其精甚真，其中有信。自古及今，其名不去。以閱眾甫。吾何以知眾甫之狀哉？以此。

Chapter twenty-one

The Body of The Tao
                    is a mist beyond your eyes

Tao of No Body,
                    and yet within it is All Creation.

Like a seed in the dark, and a dim light
    And from it, comes everything.

Root, stem, leaf . . . its essence is in everything.

Everything is born from this Tao
                    I say so, and I can prove it!

From the beginning of time until now
the Tao is eternal *because it is Creation.*

How do I know the Tao is the root of all being?

Because
            I know this.

Chapter twenty-two

Learn to yield and be soft
If you want to survive.

Learn to bow
And you will stand in your full height.

Learn to empty yourself
                              and be filled by the Tao

. . . the way a valley empties itself into a river.

Use up all you are
And then you can be made new.

Learn to have nothing
And you will have everything.

Sages always act like this,
and are Children of the Tao.

Never trying to impress, their being shines forth
Never saying 'this is it', people see what the truth is –

Never boasting, they leave the space they can be valued in
And never claiming to be who they are, people can see them

And since they never argue, no one argues with them either . . .

So the ancient ones say
                              'Bend, and you will rule'.

Is this a lie? You'll find it is true.

Be true to yourself, and all will go well with you.

二十二章

曲則全，枉則直，窪則盈，敝則新，少則得，多則惑。

是以聖人抱一爲天下式。不自見，故明。不自是，故彰。不自伐，故有功。不自矜，故長。夫唯不爭，故天下莫能與之爭。古之所謂"曲則全"者，豈虛言哉！誠全而歸之。

Chapter twenty-three

It is a natural thing
　　　　to talk sparingly.

And surely, this is right – because even a great wind
and lashing rain do not go on forever.

It is naturally so. Both Heaven and Earth know it.

And if neither can hold on to such an outpouring for long
what makes people think they can?

If you follow the Tao,
　　　　all you do will belong to it.

If you act with Virtue,
All you do will have its power.

If you lose these –
Then everyway you will be lost.

If you go the Way of Tao, it can only be with you.
If you go the Way of Virtue, its purity will sustain you.

But if you go the way of loss, then that will be your name;
And if you cannot trust, no one will trust you.

故從事於道者，道者同於道。德者同於德。失者同於失。
同於道者，亦樂得之。同於德者德，亦樂得之。同於失者失，亦樂得
之。信不足焉，有不信焉。

二十三章

希言自然。故飄風不終朝，驟雨不終日。孰為此者？天地。天地尚不能久，而況於人乎？

二十四章

企者不立。跨者不行。自見者不明。自是者不彰。自伐者無功。自矜者不長。

其在道也曰：「餘食贅物，或惡之。故有道者不處。」

72

Chapter twenty-four

A man on tiptoe

can't walk easily.

The man who strides on ahead is bound to tire.

The kind of person who always insists
on his way of seeing things
can never learn anything from anyone.

Those who always want to be seen
will never help others to be.

The showman is never
secretly respected by anyone.

People like these, say the Wise Ones
are as useless as the left-over food at a feast:

No true follower can relate to them.

Chapter twenty-five

Before the world was

   And the sky was filled with stars . . .

There was

         a strange, unfathomable Body.

This Being, this Body is silent

         and beyond all substance and sensing.

It stretches beyond everything

            spanning the empyrean.

It has always been here, and it always will be.

Everything comes from it, and then

               it is the Mother of Everything.

I do not know its name. So I call it TAO.

I am loath to call it 'greater than everything',
but it is.

And being greater, it infuses all things

           moving far out and returning to the Source.

Tao is Great,

        Tao, the Great!

It is greater than Heaven,
Greater than the Earth –
Greater than the king.

These are the four great things,
and the ruler is the least of them.

Humanity is schooled by the Earth;

Earth is taught by Heaven,

And Heaven is guided by the Tao.

And the Tao

         goes with what is absolutely natural.

二十五章

有物混成，先天地生。寂兮寥兮！獨立不改，周行而不殆。可以為天下母。吾不知其名，字之曰「道」。強為之名曰大。大曰逝。逝曰遠。遠曰反。故道大，天大，地大，王亦大。域中有四大，而王居其一焉。人法地，地法天，天法道，道法自然。

75

Chapter twenty-six

What holds, what you can trust
Is the same as this quietness –
And it is light-hearted.

This quiet light-hearted silence
Is the key to being free from emotion.

The sage never abandons the Tao,
He never lets its weight out of his sight.

He may live in a fabulous house
But he never gets caught up wanting to –

And though there are always temptations,
He stays unswayed, and smiles.

So why is it that our rulers
Seem so bright, but are
Glib and insubstantial?

Losing the weight of the Tao
Means you lose your root;

And when you can't sit still
You lose
                    the source.

重爲輕根，靜爲躁君。是以聖人終日行不離輜重。雖有榮觀，燕處超然。

奈何萬乘之主，而以身輕天下？輕則失本，躁則失君。

二十六章

Chapter twenty-seven

The sage who goes by the way leaves no traces
The sage who speaks the true law never slips up –
He never calculates what profit he can make from what he does..

He keeps out thieves with wisdom! He's never robbed –
He makes sure the rules are binding, then no one can undo them:

He is aware of everyone, leaving no one uncounted;
He cares like a parent, and wastes nothing.

This is the essence of harmony.

So, a good man is a model for a bad one
And, misguided, he is touched by his goodness.

Not to follow a teacher here
Or to love his precious message
Is to lose the Way, however clever you are –

This is the essence of the matter.

善行無轍迹。善言無瑕讁。善數不用籌策。善閉無關楗而不可開。

二十七章

善結無繩約而不可解。

是以聖人常善救人，故無棄人，常善救物，故無棄物。是謂襲明。

故善人者，不善人之師。不善人者，善人之資。不貴其師，不愛其

資，雖智大迷。是謂要妙。

二十八章

知其雄，守其雌，為天下谿，為天下谿，常德不離，復歸於嬰兒。
知其白，守其黑，為天下式。為天下式，常德不忒，復歸於無極。
知其榮，守其辱，為天下谷。常德乃足，復歸於樸。樸散則為器。
聖人用之則為官長，故大制不割。

80

Chapter twenty-eight

Understand the thrust of the yang –
But be more like the yin in your being.

Be like a valley
              that parts to its stream;
Be like a stream
               for the earth . . .
And channel it,
              so it flows – to the sea.

Be newborn – be free of yourself,
be humble,
          be earthy,
                 be a valley for the whole world.

Be a channel for the energies here –
weave them in a true and practical way
so they can link up with the Way and become one again.

Oneness generates everything:

When the sage rules in the light of it,
He rules everything.

A wise man never tries to break up the Whole.

Chapter twenty-nine

If a ruler behaves as if he's invented the world,
He will do no good at all.

The earth is a sacred vessel —

            and it cannot be owned or improved.

If you try to possess it, you will destroy it:
If you try to hold on to it — you will lose it.

Some are leaders, then, and others follow.
Some drift like the wind, and others drive hard.
Some are thick-skinned, and others have no armour;
And some are the destroyers, and others they destroy.

So now you know why

        the sage abandons greed,
        all false charm —
        and every last iota of pride.

二十九章

將欲取天下而為之，吾見其不得已。天下神器，不可為也。為者敗之，執者失之。

故物或行或隨，或歔或吹，或強或羸，或挫或隳。是以聖人去甚，去奢去泰。

善者果而已，不敢以取強。果而勿矜。果而勿伐。果而勿驕。果而不得已。果而勿強。物壯則老，是謂不道，不道早已。

Chapter thirty

以道佐人主者，不以兵強天下。其事好還。師之所處，荊棘生焉。大軍之後，必有凶年。

三十章

The Emperor's advisors will never recommend violence
if they know what the Tao is.
If you use the strategy of warfare
it can only result in revenge.

After troops have tramped by
only weeds and nettles grow in the broken ground.
There can be no harvest,
and everyone is left starving.

If you need to take action, only do what is necessary.
Never abuse your power.

And if you're successful, don't be smug;
If you are a success, don't trumpet it –
If you think you've won, never overdo it –

Those who use force soon end up without it –

And this is not the Way.

And if you do not follow the Way, you will die.

The guide who walks the Way
Never resorts to violence.

The sage goes to the left side of the Emperor;
while the man of war goes to the right.

Weapons are terrible things –
and no sage will have anything to do with them,
unless there is no alternative.

The sage wants peace and quiet.

No victory is free of grief,
and so to celebrate one is to glory
in the death of innocent people.

No one who revels in death like this
can be true to the Way
or is fit to rule in our world.

At glad times, the place of honour is on the left:
after disaster, it is on the right.
So in the army, the officers stand to the left
while the general stands to the right.

So the whole thing is staged like a funeral.

When a war kills many, we must mourn for them –
And if you win the war, you must grieve it.

三十一章

夫佳兵者,不祥之器。物或惡之,故有道者不處。君子居則貴左,用兵則貴右。兵者不祥之器,非君子之器。不得已而用之。恬淡為上。勝而不美,而美之者,是樂殺人。夫樂殺人者,則不可以得志於天下矣。吉事尚左,凶事尚右。偏將軍居左,上將軍居右,言以喪禮處之。殺人之眾,以哀悲泣之。戰勝以喪禮處之。

87

三十二章

道常無名樸。雖小,天下莫能臣也。侯王若能守之,萬物將自賓。

天地相合,以降甘露,民莫之令而自均。

始制有名。名亦既有,夫亦將知止。知止所以不殆。譬道之在天下,猶川谷之於江海。

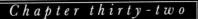
The Tao has no name

　　　　　　　it is a cloud that has no shape.

If a ruler
follows it faithfully,
then every living thing under heaven will say yes to him.

Heaven and earth make love,
And a sweet dew-rain falls.
The people do not know why,
But they are gathered together like music.

Things have been given names from the beginning.
We need to know when we have enough names: this is wisdom.

At the beginning of time
The sage gave names to everything – seen, and unseen.

A ruler who walks the Way
Is like a river reaching the sea
Gathering the waters of the streams

　　　　　　　　　　into himself,

　　　as he goes.

Chapter thirty-three

知人者智。自知者明。勝人者有力。自勝者強。知足者富。強行者有志。不失其所者久。死而不亡者壽。

三十三章

When you know the true being of another,
You can judge –

And if you truly know the Tao
                    you will be in the light.

It takes force to control people:
but if I am humble, I can never be overcome.

If you know what you have is enough
you will be satisfied.

But if you think you don't have enough
then you will never have enough!

If you follow the Tao, what you are will last.

You will live, and live, and outlive yourself again.

三十四章

大道氾兮，其可左右。萬物恃之而生而不辭，功成不名有，衣養萬物而不爲主。常無欲，可名於小。萬物歸焉，而不爲主，可名爲大。以其終不自爲大，故能成其大。

Chapter thirty-four

The Great Tao goes everywhere
 past your left hand and your right –

 filling the whole of space.

It is breath to every thing, and yet it asks for nothing back;
It feeds and creates everything, but it will never tell you so.

It nurtures all things
 without lording it over anything.

It names itself in the lowest of the low.

It holds what it makes,
Yet never fights to do so:

that is why we call it Great.

 Why? Because it never tries to be so.

Chapter thirty-five

Everyone will gather to the man
Who rules in the light of the One.

To trust such a being is to live
In true happiness and healing.

Good food and sweet music
May make you stop –
You listen, in passing.

But the Tao: how does it seem?
Oh, tasteless and shapeless by comparison.

You cannot even hear it.
Is it even worth trying to?

Yes, my friend
                    because it is unending.

執大象，天下往。往而不害，安平太。樂與餌，過客止。道之出口，淡乎其無味，視之不足見，聽之不足聞，用之不可既。

三十五章

Chapter thirty-six

What is going to be diminshed
Must first be allowed to inflate.

Whatever you want to weaken
Must first be convinced of its strength.

What you want to overcome
You must first of all submit to . . .

What you want to take over
You must first of all give to –

This is called *discerning*.

You see, what is yielding and weak
Overcomes what is hard and strong:

(And just as a fish can't be seen
when he stays down in the deep

don't show your power to anyone).

三十六章

將欲歙之，必固張之。將欲弱之，必固強之。將欲廢之，必固興之。將欲奪之，必固與之。是謂微明。柔弱勝剛強。魚不可脫於淵。國之利器，不可以示人。

道常無為而無不為。侯王若能守之，萬物將自化。化而欲作，吾將鎮之以無名之樸。無名之樸，夫亦將無欲。不欲以靜天下將自定。

三十七章

Chapter thirty-seven

The Tao goes on forever
                              wu-wei — doing nothing
And yet everything gets done.

How? It does it by being,
And by being everything it does.

If people and rulers go by this
then every living thing will be well.

And if parts still want to separate
the true leader will use

                    the centrifugal weight
of this original
                    unnameable Oneness.

It is simple:

If no one wants anything for themelves
then there can be peace

and all things will know peace

the way music
                    ends in peace.

TE

德

Chapter thirty-eight

The highest kind of man
Has innate goodness,
And that is what he rules with.

The lesser man brags about how good he is –
And isn't much good, I can tell you.

A Man of Te rules by *wu-wei*
Doing nothing for himself or of himself.

The lesser man acts from his ego
And what he wants is gratification.

A man who rules with compassion
Acts through it – and no one even realizes.

A legal man acts judiciously
But he is still serving his own ends.

And the rigid man uses laws
And if people don't like it, force.

If the true Tao is lost

then morality takes its place.

禮為之，而莫之應，則攘臂而扔之。

故失道而後德，失德而後仁，失仁而後義，失義而後禮。夫禮者，

忠信之薄，而亂之首。前識者道之華，而愚之始。是以大丈夫

處其厚，不居其薄，處其實，不居其華。故棄彼取此。

老子道德經　下篇

三十八章

上德不德，是以有德。下德失德，是以無德。上德無為，而無以為。

下德為之，而有以為。上仁為之，而無以為。上義為之，而有以為。上

If that fails, we have 'conscience'.
When that fades, we get 'justice'.

When that disappears, we have the *status quo*.

Confusion reigns. No one knows
what's going on. Forecasts
and prophecies abound –
and they are merely a gloss on the Tao,
they are the root of all
twisted guidance.

So the sage only looks at what is really real.
He doesn't just look at the surface –
He blows away the dust and drinks the water . . .
He doesn't just go for the flower
But also for the roots and the fruit.

Blow away the dust, now:
Come to the living water.

Chapter thirty-nine

故致數輿無輿。不欲琭琭如玉，珞珞如石。

為本邪？非乎？

故貴以賤為本，高以下為基。是以侯王自謂孤寡不穀，此非以賤

高將恐蹶。

From its first days, the universe came from the One:
The heavens are one, and clear, and round because of it
The earth is one, and is its firm infused foundation . . .
The spirit force is one, with all it brings into being –
The valley is a oneness, and so it flows and renews all things,
Everything is one – every living thing is one, and alive!
Kings and lords are one in a kingdom that is one:
And they can only rule truly because of the One.

If Heaven wasn't clear, then the sky would fall down.
If the earth cannot be peaceful, it will tear itself apart.
If the Spirit cannot bless, then no one will believe in it –
If the valley can't rebirth, then the valley will run dry.
If life can't be itself, then life will be nothing:
And if the king is nothing, then the world will be at war.

Everything has both yin and yang in it –

        and from their rise-and-fall-coupling comes new life.

三十九章

昔之得一者：天得一以清。地得一以寧。神得一以靈、谷得一以盈。萬物得一以生。侯王得一以為天下貞。

其致之，天無以清，將恐裂。地無以寧，將恐發。神無以靈、將恐歇。谷無以盈，將恐竭。萬物無以生，將恐滅。侯王無以貴

The highest authority needs the basement as its base,
And the depths are the foundation of the heights.

That is why rulers call themselves lonely,
like souls in a wilderness who have no home.
And, in doing so, don't they see then
that their roots lie with the people?

To see yourself as extraordinary
is to stand out like jade among ordinary stones;

but what people ignore – the lonely, and the worthless –
is the rock a true leader finds himself on.

You see, you win by losing – and you lose by succeeding.

四十章

反者道之動，弱者道之用。
天下萬物生扵有。有生扵無。

The Tao moves
          in every direction at once –
its essence is fluid and yielding.

It is the maker of everything under the sun:
And everything comes
                    out of nothing.

When the wisest student hears about the Tao,
He follows it without ceasing

When the average student hears about it
He follows too, but not all of the time . . .

And when the poor student gets wind of it
he laughs at it like an idiot!
And if he didn't, then it wouldn't be the Tao!

That is why the ancient ones said:

The path that is bright seems dull,
And the one who is going towards the Tao
Seems, in fact, to be going backwards –
And those who think that the Way is easy
Will find it extremely hard.

The greatest virtue is to be empty like a valley.
Those who think they are perfect never are –
those who feel that they are feel inadequate to the task,
and morals seem to be no more than a contrivance.

大方無隅。大器晚成。大音希聲。大象無形。道隱無名。

夫唯道。善貸且成。

四十一章

上士聞道，勤而行之。中士聞道，若存若亡。下士聞道，大笑之。
不笑不足以為道。

故建言有之：「明道若昧。進道若退。夷道若纇」。

上德若谷。大白若辱，廣德若不足。建德若偷。質真若渝。

A great square has no corners:
A great work is never done with;
A great shout comes from a whisper,
And the greatest of forms
                                    is beyond shape.

Tao without substance –
Invisible –
Ever-creating

Forever creating

Chapter forty-two

The Tao

gives birth to the One:

The One

gives birth to the two;

The Two

give birth to the three –

The Three give birth to every living thing.

All things are held in yin, and carry yang:

And they are held together in the *ch'i* of teeming energy.

四十二章

道生一。一生二。二生三。三生萬物。萬物負陰而抱陽。沖氣以為和。

人之所惡，唯孤寡不穀，而王公以為稱。故物，或損之而益，或益之而損。

人之所教，我亦教之。『強梁者，不得其死。』吾將以為教父。

四十三章

天下之至柔，馳騁天下之至堅，無有入無間。吾是以知無為之有益。不言之教，無為之益，天下希及之。

Chapter forty-three

The very softest thing of all
   can ride like a galloping horse
      through the hardest of things.

Like water, like water penetrating rock.
And so the invisible enters in.

That is why I know it is wise
   to act by doing nothing.
And how few, how very few understand this!

People teach in the world
what I know to be true:

if you live violently

      that is how you will die.

Chapter forty-four

What really matters most,
Your image or your soul?
    What do you care about
Your money, or your life?
    What's actually the best,
Making it – or losing?

If you pour all your energy into one thing,
You're sure to harm the rest of your being
And if you invest it all in profit –
You'll end up losing the whole lot.

If you're not always wanting, you can be at peace.
And if you're not always trying to be someone
You can be who you really are

                    and go the whole way.

四十四章

名與身就親？身與貨就多？得與亡就病？
是故甚愛必大費，多藏必厚亡。
知足不辱。知止不殆。可以長久。

四十五章

大成若缺其不弊。大盈若沖,其用不窮。大真若屈。大巧若拙。

大辯若訥。

躁勝寒。靜勝熱,清靜為天下正。

Chapter forty-five

A great thing done is never perfect –
But that doesn't mean it fails: it does what it is.

Real richness means to act as if you had nothing,
Because then you will never be drained of it.

The greatest straightness seems bent,
The greatest ability seems awkward,
And the greatest speech, like a stammering.

Act calmly, not coldly.
Peace is greater than anger.
Tranquillity and harmony

        are the true order of things.

Chapter forty-six

'When the Tao runs the world,
the horses work the farms.'

Without Tao

the horses are led into war along the borders.

You see, if people want more and more
it can only lead to disaster.

Greed

is the seed of apocalypse –
it is the rocket-fuel of selfishness:
me, me, me!

If people could only be glad with all they have,
if they only knew it, they'd be happy.

四十六章

天下有道，卻走馬以糞。天下無道，戎馬生於郊。

禍莫大於不知足。咎莫大於欲得。故知足之足常足矣。

四十七章

不出戶，知天下。不闚牖，見天道。其出彌遠，其知彌少。是以聖人不行而知，不見而名，不為而成。

Chapter forty-seven

Without going anywhere,

      you can know the whole world.

Without even opening your window,

      you can know the ways of Heaven.

You see: the further away you go, the less you know . . .

The sage doesn't need to travel around:
Why? Because he can still understand.

He sees without needing 'to see',
He never does anything, and yet

                 it all happens.

Chapter forty-eight

Usually, people read because they want to know –
but the more you study the Tao, the less you want knowledge.

And as you want less and less, you come closer to not-doing.
Wu-wei – this is the way to get things done.

The best way to run the world
                              is to let it take its course
– and to get yourself
                    out of the way of it!

四十八章

為學日益，為道日損，損之又損，以至於無為。無為而無不為。取天下常以無事。及其有事，不足以取天下。

123

四十九章

聖人無常心，以百姓心為心。善者吾善之，不善者吾亦善之，德善。信者吾信之，不信者吾亦信之，德信。聖人在天下，歙歙為天下渾其心。百姓皆注其耳目。聖人皆孩之。

Chapter forty-nine

'The sage is never opinionated,
He listens to the mind of the people.'

I am kind to people when they are kind to me.
I am kind to them even if they hate me.
Virtue – *te* – is its own reward.

I trust those who trust me,
I also trust those who have no faith in me:
What I give, I receive.

A sage is self-effacing and mindful of offence.
He sets himself as his own example.
How shall I treat you, my son?

Like a child.

Chapter fifty

In the normal way of things
every three in ten live long,
while every three in ten die young —
and for those just passing through their lives
(that is, every three in ten) the chances are the same.

Why is this?
Well, it all depends on how identified
they are with the mundane world of matter.

People who know how to live
will never do things that threaten their lives,
any more than a traveller who knows
will run into a tiger or a wild buffalo.

Living well is like wearing
a kind of armour that nothing can penetrate.

Living badly is like being attacked!

A practised sage is invulnerable to attacks
that punch like a buffalo's horn,
that claw like a leaping tiger —
or that stab like a knife in the back.

And why is this?

Because he is impeccable.

五十章

出生入死。生之徒有十三。死之徒有十三。人之生，動之死地，亦有十三。夫何故？以其生生之厚。

蓋聞善攝生者，陸行不遇兕虎，入軍不被甲兵。兕無所投其角，虎無所措其爪。兵無所容其刃。夫何故？以其無死地。

五十一章

道生之，德畜之，物形之，勢成之。是以萬物莫不尊道而貴德。

道之尊，德之貴，夫莫之命而常自然。

故道生之，德畜之，長之，育之，亭之，毒之，養之，覆之。

生而不有，爲而不恃，長而不宰。是謂玄德。

Chapter fifty-one

Everything streams from the Tao,

Everything is nurtured by Te

Everything is made out of substance.

Everything is created by the Tao of Nature
– and from everything on earth that surrounds it.

So every living thing
should bow to the Tao,
the Tao and its Virtue

because they are what it is.

Everything that breathes comes from the Tao,
And the Virtue feeds and takes care of it.

They grace things without possessing them,
They benefit everything but ask for nothing back,
They give themselves into everything without seeking control.

This is the essence
of the original intention.

Chapter fifty-two

Every living thing

Comes from the Mother of Us All:

If we can understand the Mother
Then we can understand her children;

And if we know ourselves as children
We can see the source is Her.

And, well, if your body dies –
there's nothing to be frightened about.

If you keep your mouth shut
And stay inside –
Then you'll live a long time.

If you blurt out
What you think to everyone,
Then you won't last long.

Value littleness. This is wisdom.

To bend like a reed
                                    in the wind
– that is real strength.

Use your mind, but stay close to the light
And it will lengthen its glow
                                    right through your life.

五十二章

天下有始，以為天下母。既得其母，以知其子。既知其子，復守其母，沒身不殆。

塞其兌，閉其門，終身不勤。開其兌，濟其事，終身不救。

見小曰明，守柔曰強。用其光，復歸其明，無遺身殃，是為習常。

五十三章

使我介然有知，行於大道，唯施是畏。大道甚夷，而民好徑。

朝甚除，田甚蕪，倉甚虛；服文綵，帶利劍，厭飲食，財貨有餘。

是謂夸盜，非道也哉！

Chapter fifty-three

If all I know is a fraction –
then my only fear is of losing the thread . . .

The Great Way is easy
but people are forever being taken down sidetracks.

They look after the palaces,
But ignore the fields!

The granaries are empty
– but they wear wonderful clothes!

They go about with arms
and gorge themselves on fine food and drink.

How rich they are –
and they have stolen it all from the poor.

They are the robber barons of now –

This is not the real Tao!

Chapter fifty-four

What is built on rock

                     cannot be pulled down;

What is held lightly

                can never be lost.

Meditate on virtue within yourself,
and you will find the benefit of virtue.

Use it as the ground for the family,
and your virtue will last for generations.

Take it as your guidance for the village,
and the place will blossom for years to come.

Use it to guide the nation,
and that nation will create abundance.

Be guided by it for the Whole,
and it will flood its way over the world.

So, look at someone else as you would yourself
And treat other families as you would your own;
See your community in other communities,
Think of all countries as part of your being
And treasure the world as the round centre of everything.

How can I see the world like this?
Because I have eyes.

五十四章

善建者不拔。善抱者不脫。子孫以祭祀不輟。

修之於身，其德乃真。修之於家，其德乃餘。修之於鄉，其德乃長。修之於國，其德乃豐，修之於天下，其德乃普。

故以身觀身，以家觀家，以鄉觀鄉，以國觀國，以天下觀天下。

吾何以知天下然哉？以此。

五十五章

含德之厚，比於赤子。蜂蠆虺蛇不螫。猛獸不據，攫鳥不搏。骨弱筋柔而握固。未知牝牡之而全作，精之至也。終日號而不嗄，和之至也。

知和曰常。知常曰明。益生曰祥。心使氣曰強。物壯則老，謂之不道。不道早已。

'Those who have true *te*
Are like a newborn baby.'

– and if they seem like this, they will not be stung
by wasps or snakes, or pounced on
by animals in the wild or birds of prey.

A baby is weak and supple, but his hand can grasp your finger.
He has no desire as yet, and yet he can be erect –
he can cry day and night without even getting hoarse
such is the depth of his harmony.

It's stupid to rush around.
When you fight against yourself, it shows in your face.
But if you draw your sap

                    from your heart
then you will be truly strong.

You will be great.

Chapter fifty-six

If you know what it is, don't talk it away:
If you do, then you don't understand.

Hush, keep it in, and your doorway shut –
Steer clear of sharpness and untangle the knots.

Feel your lightness and let it merge with others,
This, we say, is our basic oneness.

The sage who does this doesn't have to worry
about people called 'friends' or 'enemies',
with profit or loss, honour or disgrace –

He is a Master of Life, instead.

五十六章

知者不言。言者不知。

塞其兌，閉其門，挫其銳，解其分，和其光，同其塵，是謂玄同。

故不可得而親，不可得而疏；不可得而利，不可得而害；不可得而貴，不可得而賤。故為天下貴。

以正治國

五十七章

以正治國,以奇用兵,以無事取天下,吾何以知其然哉?以此;天下多忌諱,而民彌貧,民多利器,國家滋昏。人多伎巧,奇物滋起。法令滋彰,盜賊多有。

故聖人云:「我無為而自化。我好靜而民自正。我無事而民自富。我無欲而民自樸。」

Chapter fifty-seven

To rule a nation, use justice
To win a battle – cunning,
But remember: *wu-wei* is the only true way.
How do I know this?
I will explain:

The more rules you have, the more unhappy people are;
And the more weapons there are, the worse things happen.
The more we want luxuries, the more we abandon simplicity –
And the more laws you pass, the more we will break them.

So the sage says: I do nothing, and the people come together;
By leaving them alone I let them be on the path –
By not using my power, they become rich in themselves.
And if I want nothing, they will return to the essence of their being.

Chapter fifty-eight

'If you govern with a generous hand –
        then your people will be good people.
But if your system is too constricting
        then your people will outwit you . . .'

Good fortune, we say, can come from disaster:
And the reverse is true as well.

Who knows where all this will lead?

Honesty can flip into deceit in a moment,
People trying to be good can fall into the dark
And it can take them years to get out of it.

So the sage is like a razor, but he doesn't cut
He is straight as a die, but not pointedly so –
He is bright, but not blindingly so . . .

五十八章

其政悶悶，其民淳淳。其政察察，其民缺缺。禍兮福之所倚，福兮禍之所伏。誰知其極？其無正，正復為奇。善復為妖。人之迷，其日固久。是以聖人方而不割，廉而不劌，直而不肆，光而不耀。

五十九章

治人事天，莫若嗇。夫唯嗇，是謂早服。早服謂之重積德。重積德，則無不克。無不克，則莫知其極，可以有國。有國之母，可以長久。是謂深根固柢，長生久視之道。

Chapter fifty-nine

When ruling the world and serving Heaven,
The sage uses simplicity in everything he does.

Simplicity comes from letting go of what you want.

If you've been true to yourself earlier in your life
Then *te* builds up in you like a well that never fails.
Nothing is impossible, then – and nothing can stop you.
And if you have no limits – then you can hold the State.

If the sage can find the Mother of a Nation
Then he will govern for a long, long time.

All this comes from his rootedness in the Tao,
The Tao of Ages, the Mountain Of Vision And Of Wings.

Chapter sixty

六十章

治大國若烹小鮮。以道莅天下，其鬼不神。非其鬼不神，其神不傷人，非其神不傷人，聖人亦不傷人，夫兩不相傷，故德交歸焉。

Ruling a big country
Is like cooking a small fish:
You have to handle it with care.

If a sage uses the Tao
Then evil forces have no power:
He doesn't harm people either.

Through *te*, you see
We have harmony.

六十一章

大國者下流。天下之交，天下之牝。牝常以靜勝牡，以靜爲下。故大國以下小國，則取小國。小國以下大國，則取大國。故或下以取，或下而取。大國不過欲兼畜人，小國不過欲入事人，夫兩者各得其所欲大者，宜爲下。

Chapter sixty-one

A great country is like a low-lying estuary −
It is a place where all the lesser streams mingle and merge.

Everything comes together there . . .

And a woman wins her man: how does she do it?
By using the power of her yin like an anchor,
A still deep bowl
               into which it all flows.

This is passiveness.

So if a great country takes a low place
It wins over the trust of a smaller state;
And if a small country shows humility
It wins the trust of a whole nation.

And it's like this: those who want to win must yield,
And those who are yielding should stay where they are.

A great country needs to grow:
A small one needs protection.

That way, everyone gets what they want −

            when the greater learns to be below.

Chapter sixty-two

The Tao
            is the source of 'the ten thousand things',

It is the sage's priceless pearl,

And it redeems
                everything.

You know, people like to use nice words to impress you.
People act nicely to gain your respect –
but even if a person is bad,
neither the sage nor the Tao will desert him. They accept him.

And when the Emperor is crowned and the three ministers appointed,
it's better to stay where you are and be with the Tao
than to hurry off with gifts of jade and a team of four horses.

The old ones 'knew this gesture',
and by ruling this way they were never
guilty of transgressions or errors.

Nothing under Heaven matters more

                        than this kind of knowing.

六十二章

道者萬物之奧，善人之寶，不善人之所保。
美言可以市尊。行可以加人。人之不善，何棄之有？
故立天子，置三公，雖有拱璧，以先駟馬，不如坐進此道。
古之所以貴此道者何？不曰以求得，有罪以免邪？故為
天下貴。

天下難事必作於易。天下大事必作於細，是以聖人終不為大，故能成其大。夫輕諾必寡信。多易必多難。是以聖人猶難之，故終無難矣。

Chapter sixty-three

爲無爲。事無事。味無味。大小多少。報怨以德。圖難於其

易。爲大於其細。

六十三章

The sage does nothing, and so he never fails –
He holds on to nothing, and so he never loses . . .
Whereas the rest of us always seem to mess up our lives
just at the moment when we seem to be succeeding!

That's why the sage wants nothing for himself.
He doesn't want precious things or possessions.
What is he? A Student Of The Unknowable,
so he doesn't make mistakes like the rest of us
but always tries to help us to be true to who we are
without ever standing in our way.

And so he says: do things *wu-wei*, by doing nothing
Achieve without trying to achieve anything –
Savour the taste of what you cannot taste

Make a small thing great, and the few into many –
Take on the largest things when they're still small,
Start the hardest things while they're still easy.

It's always the person who thinks things are easy
that finds them the hardest in the end.

The way he sees it: everything's potentially tricky,
so he never ends up out of his depth.

六十四章

其安易持。其未兆易謀。其脆易泮。其微易散。為之於未有，治之於未亂。

合抱之木，生於毫末。九層之臺，起於累土。千里之行，始於足下。

為者敗之，執者失之。是以聖人無為故無敗，無執故無失。

民之從事，常於幾成而敗之。慎終而始，則無敗事。

是以聖人欲不欲，不貴難得之貨；學不學，復眾人之所過，以輔萬物之自然而不敢為。

Chapter sixty-four

When everything is peaceful, don't forget the danger;
When things are safe, don't lose your edge –
A brittle thing can break
                              easily
And a small thing fragment.

So 'act before it happens'.
'order things before chaos breaks out'.

A great tree which takes a crowd to span its base
Started from being a tiny seed;
And a tower nine sections high began in the ground.

A journey of a thousand miles starts with the first step.

To act as if you know it all is catastrophic:
and if you try to control it

            you will stare into your empty hand.

六十五章

古之善為道者，非以明民，將以愚之。民之難治，以其智多。故以智治國，國之賊。不以智治國，國之福。知此兩者亦稽式。常知稽式，是謂玄德。玄德深矣，遠矣，與物反矣，然後乃至大順。

Chapter sixty-five

In ancient times, the shrewdest rulers
Didn't try to give people too much know-how.

What did they do? They kept them living simply.
So why are people so difficult to govern now?
Because they know too much in their so-called freedom.

If a leader works deviously,
He will turn the people against him – look and see.
But if you refuse to use that kind of knowing,
Your people will be blessed and happy.

This is where two streams divide:

And if you rule this way
You will be walking the great path of Te.

Deep Te – this Virtue is everywhere

drawing us all
                              into our final destiny:

                    Oneness Of The Source And The Sea . . .

六十六章

江海所以能為百谷王者，以其善下之，故能為百谷王。

是以欲上民必以言下之，欲先民必以身後之。

是以聖人處上而民不重，處前而民不害。是以天下樂推而不厭。以其不爭，故天下莫能與之爭。

Chapter sixty-six

Why is the sea

        the king of a hundred tributaries?

Because everything comes down to it —
   So it is kingly
By this name.

So a sage that wants to rule the people must be below them.
If he wants to be their leader, he must be behind them.

If he has no desire to control

        then the people will not feel oppressed;

And if he stands before them for their own sake, and not his

        they will not harm him.

Trusted by everyone, no one will tire of him.

What is his secret?
   He never competes.
So there is no one else

        but him.

天下皆謂我道大，似不肖。夫唯大，故似不肖。若肖，久矣其細也夫。

我有三寶，持而保之。一曰慈。二曰儉。三曰不敢為天下先。慈故能勇。儉故能廣。不敢為天下先，故能成器長。

今舍慈且勇，舍儉且廣，舍後且先，死矣。

夫慈以戰則勝，以守則固。天將救之，以慈衛之。

Chapter sixty-seven

I have three priceless treasures:
The first is Compassion

the second, thrift

And the third is that I never want to be ahead of you.

If I have compassion, you will die for me. I know that.
If I waste nothing, I can give myself to you all –
And if I don't seem perfect, then you'll trust me to lead you.

These days people scorn compassion. They try to be tough.
They spend all they have, and yet want to be generous
They despise humility, and want to be the best.

I tell you that way is Death's.

If you have loved your people, you will know it
they will fight tooth and nail for you in attack or defence.

This is the protection of Heaven, and your harvest.

六十八章

善為士者不武。善戰者不怒。善勝敵者不與。善用人者為之下。是謂不爭之德。是謂用人之力。是謂配天古之極。

Chapter sixty-eight

A canny soldier never provokes anyone,
And is never made to lose his temper.

A good fighter never confronts his enemy head-on:
And those who know how to handle people do it humbly.

This comes from the virtue of not-striving,
and from knowing how to link with other people's energy.

Since time gone in the mists

       this has been the way to 'pair up' with Heaven.

六十九章

用兵有言：「吾不敢為主而為客，不敢進寸而退尺。」是謂行無行。攘無臂，扔無敵，執無兵。

禍莫大於輕敵，輕敵幾喪吾寶。故抗兵相加，哀者勝矣。

Chapter sixty-nine

There is a saying, you know, which soldiers have:

'I never use my force before my enemy uses his.
I'd sooner go back a foot than advance an inch.'

This is called going forward without moving,
Rolling up your sleeve without showing your arm –
And by not, you defeat him without apparently doing anything.

This is like being armed, but no one sees what you have.

Never think your enemy is feeble. That's disastrous.

If I do that, I'm bound to lose all I have!

So, you see, when the battle begins
It is the one who seems weakest that will win.

Chapter seventy

My words are really very easy to understand
And be with, and walk in . . . but no one can!

My words have roots, my actions have precedents
But people don't see this, and so they don't see me.

So few of you know or understand me
And so the Tao becomes ever more important . . .

The sage goes round like a supertramp,
Hiding the jade, the jewel he carries in his inmost heart.

七十章

吾言甚易知，甚易行。天下莫能知，莫能行。言有宗。事有君。夫唯無知，是以不我知。知我者希，則我者貴。是以聖人被褐懷玉。

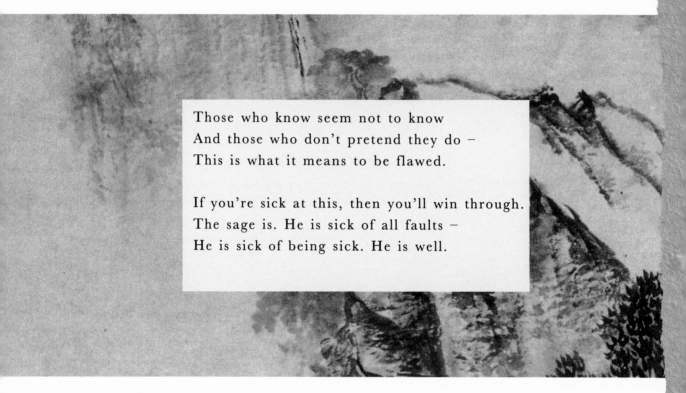

Those who know seem not to know
And those who don't pretend they do –
This is what it means to be flawed.

If you're sick at this, then you'll win through.
The sage is. He is sick of all faults –
He is sick of being sick. He is well.

知不知，上。不知知，病。夫唯病病，是以不病。聖人不病，以其病

七十一章

病，是以不病。

民不畏威，則大威至。無狎其所居。無厭其所生。夫唯不厭，是以不厭。

七十二章

是以聖人自知不自見，自愛不自貴。故去彼取此。

When the people lack a sense of awe,
There is bound to be disorder or disaster.

Never oppress them in their own homes,
or interfere with their means of livelihood.

If you don't oppose them,
They won't try to depose you.

So, the sage who really knows himself
never shows himself off to his people –
loves himself, without false pride –

discards the mask, and wears his true face.

Chapter seventy-three

A person who's brash and fearless will die,
A person who is cautious will survive –

These two are right, and they are wrong
Heaven looks down on both

                and who knows the truth?

So even the sage admits some things are beyond him.

The Tao of Heaven

              doesn't struggle, but it wins through

It doesn't ask

          yet it always hears the answer –

It doesn't demand

           yet things come, because they want to

It has no desires

        and yet everything works out as if planned.

And though the Net Of Heaven is wide,
Not even the tiniest whisper escapes it.

七十三章

勇於敢則殺，勇於不敢則活。此兩者，或利或害。天之所惡，孰知其故？是以聖人猶難之。

天之道：不爭而善勝，不言而善應，不召而自來，繟然而善謀。天網恢恢，疏而不失。

Chapter seventy-four

If the people are not afraid,
It is useless to try and scare them with death.

And if people are afraid of death
And you make a point of hanging every criminal,
Then who would dare to do anything?

Any killing must be done by an official executioner.

If someone else were to do it,
It would be like trying to copy a master carpenter –

And if you try to cut like him
you will only bloody your own hands!

常有司殺者殺。夫代司殺者殺，是謂代大匠斲。夫代大匠斲者，希有不傷其手矣。

七十四章

民不畏死，奈何以死懼之？若使民常畏死，而為奇者，吾得執而殺之，孰敢。

177

七十五章

民之饑，以其上食稅之多，是以饑。民之難治，以其上之有為，是以難治。民之輕死，以其求生之厚，是以輕死。夫無以生為者，是賢以貴生。

Chapter seventy-five

Why are the people hungry?
Because you crush them with your taxes:
That is why they have nothing.

Why are the people angry?
Because you endlessly impose your laws:
That is why they can't take any more.

And why aren't they scared of death?
Because you are voracious and you want everything.
So what have they got left to lose?

Those who only have a little
          really know how to value life.

七十六章

人之生也，柔弱。其死也，堅強。萬物草木之生也，柔脆。其死也，枯槁。故堅強者死之徒。柔弱者，生之徒。是以兵強則不勝，木強則兵。強大處下，柔弱處上。

180

Chapter seventy-six

When a body is alive, it is soft and supple
– it is cold and rigid when it dies.

When plants are alive, they are tender and trailing
– and burnt and brittle when they're dead.

What's iron hard is what is dead, then
And what is fluid and sensuous and rippling is alive . . .

And that is why a huge army
With all its strength and complacency will be defeated:
Like a great tree
                    axed down.

  Everything hard and strong will come down,
      And everything soft
                          shall rise, shall overcome.

天之道，損有餘而補不足。人之道，則不然，損不足以奉有餘。
孰能有餘以奉天下？唯有道者，是以聖人為而不恃，功成而不
處，其不欲見賢。

天之道，其猶張弓與！高者抑之，下者舉之。有餘者損之，不足者補之。

七十七章

The Tao of Heaven
　　　　　　is like the tensing of a bow:
－ what is above
　　　　　　is drawn down,
－ and what's below
　　　　　　is drawn up,
－ what has plenty is drawn from
　　　　　　and is given to what doesn't have enough.

The Heavenly Tao takes from those who have too much,
And it gives to those who have little or nothing.

Ah, but the human way is different.
Even the wealthiest leech the poor
So they can have even more.

What kind of person is it
Who has more than they need
And so gives it out, and gives it freely?

　　　　　Only a being that is filled with the Tao.

七十八章

天下莫柔弱於水，而攻堅強者莫之能勝，其無以易之。弱之勝強，

柔之勝剛，天下莫不知，莫能行。

是以聖人云：「受國之垢，是謂社稷主。受國不祥，是為天下王。」

正言若反。

Chapter seventy-eight

Nothing in the world

                    is softer than water . . .

– but we know it can wear away the hardest of things.

The supple

Overcomes the hard,

And the so-called weak, the strong.

People know this, but no one quite believes it.

The sage always shoulders the blame, and the grief

– that is why he is fit to rule

He takes on his nation like a world

As if it was the world

– and so it is.

And the truth is that the truth

                    is often a paradox . . .

七十九章

和大怨，必有餘怨。安可以為善？是以聖人執左契而不責於人。

有德司契，無德司徹。天道無親，常與善人。

Chapter seventy-nine

If you've had a real set-to with someone
And you've tried to patch it up –
And there's still some bitterness, what can you do?

I tell you: repay bitterness with good.

Those who practise Te hold credit
– but don't demand repayment.

Those who practise Virtue do their bit
– and those without it will expect you to.

The Tao of Heaven
                  doesn't deal in nepotism –
it just graces good people, like it always has and will.

Chapter eighty

If a nation could be small, with few enough people
Even if you had the means to produce more, they'd be useless.
Such a people would know that death is real,
And they wouldn't travel far, even if they were able to.
They would not vaunt their army or their weaponry.
They would count in their heads again and write by hand.
Their food would be simple, but it would feed them;
Their clothes would be fine, but homely
And they would have fires in their homes.

They would be happy with what they have!
And even though they'd live along the border within earshot
Of their neighbours' cocks at dawn, and the dogs barking,
They wouldn't mind if they never went there.

It is enough, for them, to live and let live.

八十章

小國寡民。使有什伯之器而不用。使民重死而不遠徙。雖有身輿，無所乘之。雖有甲兵，無所陳之。使人復結繩而用之。甘其食。美其服。安其居。樂其俗。鄰國相望，雞犬之聲相聞，民至老死不相往來。

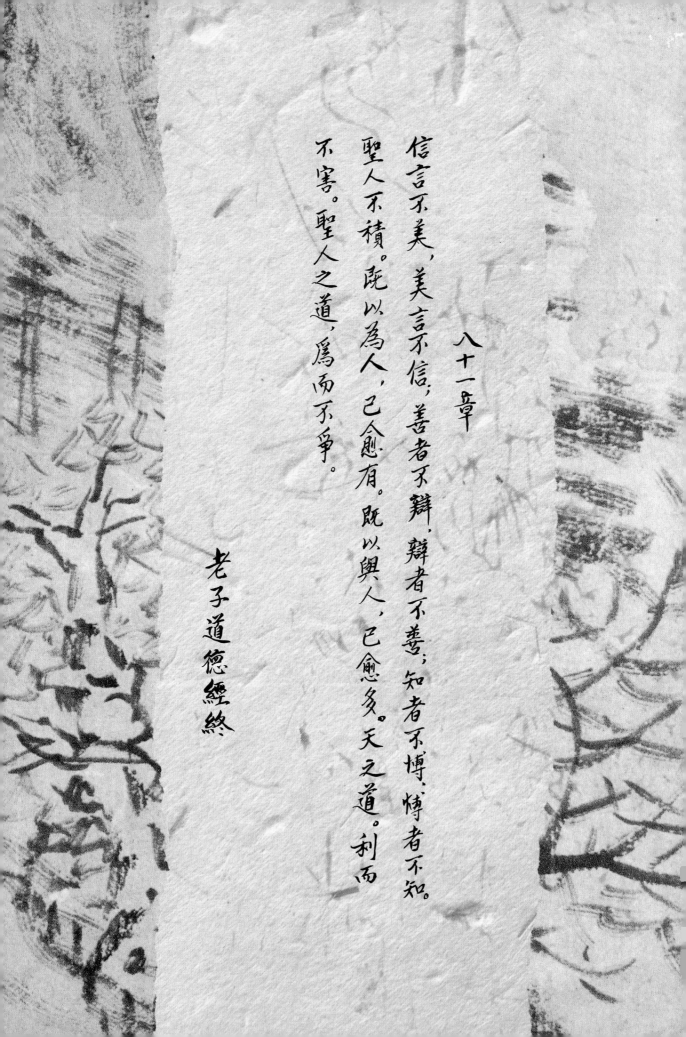

八十一章

信言不美，美言不信；善者不辯，辯者不善；知者不博，博者不知。

聖人不積。既以為人，己愈有。既以與人，己愈多。天之道，利而不害。聖人之道，為而不爭。

老子道德經終

Chapter eighty-one

No one likes the honest truth,
And all fine talk falls short of it.

Real words are never used to seduce you,
And those that do are no good.

The one who *really* knows, knows without books
– the so-called learned know nothing.

The sage holds nothing of himself back –
He uses all he has for you, and that is his reward.
He gives all he is

and that is why he's rich.

And the Tao of Heaven

feeds everything, and harms nothing

And the sage's Tao

completes it, without doing anything.

MAN-HO KWOK is the foremost
practitioner of traditional Chinese religion
in the UK. Trained for twenty years by
both Taoist and Buddhist masters in Hong
Kong, he is renowned as a scholar of
Chinese religion and, together with Martin
Palmer, has translated many ancient texts.

MARTIN PALMER, the Director of the
International Consultancy on Religion,
Education and Culture (ICOREC), is an
expert on interfaith work and author of
many books including *The Elements of
Taoism* and *Living Christianity*. He has
translated numerous ancient texts
including many from China on which he
has collaborated with Man-Ho Kwok.

JAY RAMSAY is a poet and founder of
the Chrysalis poetry project. He has
published numerous books of poetry
including his main work, *The Great Return*,
and is particularly interested in the role
of the artist-healer.